VERY FOND *of* FOOD

VERY FOND *of* FOOD

a year in recipes

Sophie Dahl

photographs by Jan Baldwin

TEN SPEED PRESS
Berkeley

For my Jamie, as everything is.

And to my grandmother, Patsy Louise, who had the courage of a lion and loved her family, along with avocados, cheap wine, and hymns.

SD

Copyright © 2011 by Sophie Dahl

All rights reserved.
Published in the United States by Ten Speed Press, an imprint of the Crown Publishing Group, a division of Random House, Inc., New York.
www.crownpublishing.com
www.tenspeed.com

Originally published in slightly different form in hardcover in Great Britain as *From Season to Season: A Year in Recipes* by HarperCollins Publishers, London, in 2011.

Ten Speed Press and the Ten Speed Press colophon are registered trademarks of Random House, Inc.

First Ten Speed Press edition, April 2012

Image on page 111 copyright © Getty Images

Library of Congress Cataloging-in-Publication Data
Dahl, Sophie, 1977-
  Very fond of food : a year in recipes / by Sophie Dahl ; photography by Jan Baldwin. — 1st American ed.
      p. cm. — (From season to season)
  Includes index.
  Summary: "A cookbook that interweaves personal anecdotes about food and the good life with 100 simple seasonal recipes"—Provided by publisher.
1. Cooking. 2. Menus. 3. Cookbooks. I. Title.
  TX714.D345 2011
  641.5—dc23
                                    2011039339

ISBN 978-1-60774-178-7
eISBN 978-1-60774-179-4

Printed in China

10 9 8 7 6 5 4 3 2 1

First American Edition

Art Director: Patrick Budge
Photographer: Jan Baldwin
Food Stylist: Alice Hart
Prop Stylist: Emma Thomas
Illustrator: Sophie Dahl
Cover Designer: Toni Tajima

Contents

Cook's notes

All pepper is freshly ground black pepper. I also like to use a coarse sea salt like Maldon.

I'm a big believer in free-range, cruelty-free products. To that end, try and buy dairy and meat from a supplier you trust, one who treats their animals with respect.

We are overfishing our painfully understocked oceans. To get a list of types of fish that are sustainable and plentiful, please go to the Marine Stewardship Council website at www.msc.org.

Stock: I use fresh or, if being lazy, Marigold Vegetable Bouillon or Kallo's Organic Free-Range Chicken Stock.

Good usefuls to have in the larder and fridge, in no particular order and given in haphazard fashion:

Belazu Balsamic Vinegar (really thick and syrupy)
Miso paste (for dressings and marinades)
Rice vinegar
Tahini
Pomegranate molasses
A good, strong mustard
Tamari
Mirin
Marsala
Horseradish root
A bunch of fresh herbs
  Tarragon
  Parsley
  Coriander
  Chives
Argan oil
Pumpkin seed oil
Some good-quality dark chocolate
Some cheap chocolate for eating on the spur of the moment or when miserable

Lemons for zesting
Chickpeas
Lentils (both Puy and yellow)
A good homemade garam masala
Star anise
Cardamom
Arborio rice
An onion
Some garlic
Pearl barley for soups and stews
Arrowroot for thickening gravies or sauces for the gluten-free
Spelt flour
Good vanilla extract
Runny honey
Fresh coffee
Stock in ice-cube trays in the freezer
Sunflower seeds to toast and add to salads and bread

Introduction

"It's a question of discipline," the little prince told me
later on. "When you've finished washing and dressing
each morning, you must tend to your planet."
Antoine de Saint-Exupéry, *The Little Prince*

In my last book, *Miss Dahl's Voluptuous Delights*, I began with writing
that many of our grandparents ate healthfully and seasonally
before there was a name for it, eating with an innate common sense
and practicality that somehow, along the way, many of us have
forgotten. This doesn't stand for everyone's grandparents, as I
discovered on a book tour to Denmark. A journalist there asked me
if I knew what her grandparents were eating fifty years ago. I knew
from her smile I was on treacherous ground and took a deep breath
of preparation.

"No," I demurred politely. "What did they eat?"

"LARD!" she said. "They lived on lard and potatoes! I eat far better
than they would have ever dreamed! What do you think of that Miss
homegrown-seasonal-vegetable-garden-have-a-walk-every-day?"

I immediately morphed into a filmic parody of Hugh Grant and
said something very English and vague like, "Well, yes, I don't know
what everyone's grandparents ate, hmm, easy to generalize, mutter,
ho hum." And blushed.

Under the gaze of watchful Danes, I stand corrected then, and speak
only for my own grandparents, who grew fruit and vegetables in their
garden, buying fish from the local fishmonger, meat from the local
butcher, and dairy from their local farmer. Every meal on their table
came to fruition with an unspoken nod to seasonality and availability.

I am keenly aware that if you are a busy working parent, or if
you live somewhere isolated, sometimes all that is on offer (or is bear-
able) is a one-stop shop. I am sometimes guilty of it myself. But I also
believe that if each one of us makes a concession towards being a
conscious consumer, we are in turn making an active contribution to
looking after our lovely planet, which has enough exterior torment
going on in it without us adding to it.

We are blessed in England to have our very definite seasons. Sometimes they feel never ending, dragging winter in particular, but the reward is tangible, both in the garden and on the plate. There is a finite certainty to the seasons that I, as a neurotic ever-pursuer of order, find blissfully predictable.

I like knowing that on a damp autumn evening, while the wind is pounding at the windows, I can transport myself with a bowl of molten comfort, a soup of squash and Parmesan, served with a thick hunk of buttered bread. This is when food meets the call of the weather, as it's hard to imagine the summer when it's been replaced by lashing rain. The memory of a ceviche, tart with lime, can propel you through the darkest days of winter, carrying you right to the moment when you can actually eat it in the garden, as drowsy bees sail past, the air throbbing with sun and lavender.

I come from a long tradition of home cooks. I write about some of them here. England is full of them, hundreds upon thousands of them practically more skilled than I. You only have to look within one of the many branches of the Women's Institute or similar to find women whose lemon bars are like the tender tears of an angel, whose puff pastry flakes with an unparalleled buttery grace. I worship at the altar of these culinary high priestesses. I still can't chop an onion properly, and my apple coring looks like the prelude to a horror film. I very occasionally make a cake that could be used as a weapon or forget to put the sugar in something. I am content with this haphazard state of affairs; it keeps me honest. I own an apple corer, and I make whoever is lurking in the kitchen around Sunday lunchtime chop my onions. I lob shards of my occasional missile cakes at the voracious crows poaching my raspberries. I happen to be a greedy writer who likes to cook and then write about what I've cooked, not a chef or a teacher. If you are looking for a voice of stern culinary authority, go elsewhere! I can give you stories, and ideas for things, along with food that is lovely, simple, and straightforward. No forgotten sugar either, I promise. This book is a collection of recipes that were either written down as they were cooked; imagined late one sleepless night and then realized, admired, and reprinted; or passed down by a stoic Norwegian great-grandmother. They are all pretty easy, with minimal fussing required. I like honest cooking that speaks for itself, cooking that begs for seconds and a satisfied smile, and I truly hope that resonates from my kitchen to yours.

In the in-between, I wish for you an army of onion choppers, sponge that is light as a feather, soufflés that defy gravity and, if all else fails, a shoulder to cry on. Cooking is not tight-lipped and mean, and it is not judgmental either. It shouldn't be, and nor should eating. Both in their very nature are providers—of nourishment, family, warmth and community, alchemy and adventure.

So whether your grandparents were lard-eating Danes, Burmese farmers, molasses-eating Mississippians, prairie-sowing Middle Americans or, like mine, a mix of staunch Scandinavian, Scottish Presbyterian, Tennessee hillbillies, and vegetable growing East Enders, most of all, I wish you happy eating. Whatever the season.

With love,
Sophie Dahl

Autumn

Autumn is all about nostalgia. For me it will forever be the season of back to school, first loves, and bonfire night. The food of autumn captures all of that in a net. Even the scent of autumn is sweet, smoky, and wistful.

From ages four to seventeen I attended quite a few schools, from the call your teacher Bob and do yoga as a sport sort, to the white gloves and curtsying to the headmistress after prayers, draconian institute that is particular to England. The one constant in the merry-go-round was the familiar feeling that flooded to the surface during the last week of August, the week before the autumn term began. It was a cross between an itch and a promise, as the evenings grew colder and supper was suddenly hot soup or a baked potato. It was furthered by buying tights and the accoutrements of junior academia: shiny pencil cases, as yet unmarred with the initials of the boy who we all had a crush on, scratched on with a compass, and virginal geometry books, so hopeful without the vivid red crosses that were sure to come.

If it was boarding school, which it was for a bit, there was the heart-plunging goodbye at the train station on a Sunday evening, the inevitable pall of rain steaming up the windows, staining the summer with a tearful goodbye. At day school, the first-day rain ceased to be a symbolic backdrop for all that was ill in the world, and more of a vanity irritant, mussing up the fringe that was so carefully straightened the night before, in honor of the sixth form boys.

Your classmates felt new like pennies, and you saw them with new eyes, at least for a day or two. Chloe now had a chest to rival Jane Russell; Joe's voice had broken and he had freckles from some faraway sun. Lola had a worldly weariness that could have something to do with a Greek waiter, and fat Robert was now thin and mean with it. Our teachers struggled with the new us, trying to gauge our emotional temperature with the old jokes that used to work, before we went and grew quietly behind their backs. So much can happen in ten weeks. Long gone from school, I still know that much can shift in a summer.

Maybe this is why autumn makes me so nostalgic. The tangible chrysalis effect of what's changed. I watch it now with my younger cousins and the children of friends. Fun fairs and postgraduation nights of camping in places that parents would balk at, sangria and sunburn, and thinking you're in love with a person who can barely say hello in your language. Discovering that some friends won't, as you thought, walk into adult life with you, that all of those nights spent whispering secrets when the lights were out will be instead relegated to the yellowing pages of a diary.

During the summer I was in Los Angeles, far, far away from the thought of rain, tights, or cozy autumnal food. I stayed at my aunt's house, which was filled with kids home from college for the summer and her menagerie of animals, including a bowl of violently colored jellyfish and Frances Bacon, her potbellied pig. Frances is of variable temper, enormous, and partially blind; she hates babies and cats in no particular order. She is very fond of strawberries, bed, and sitting on the dogs, who live in mortal fear of her. We have always got on reasonably well. This all changed when my aunt went away for a week. Although I did all the things Frances likes—scratching her ears, rubbing sunscreen on her broad scaly back, feeding her banana skins, and tucking her in at night—I think she connected my arrival with my aunt's disappearance and decided, like an errant stepchild, to make my life complicated. She crept stealthily into the larder (my favorite place) and trapped me there daily, blocking my exit with her two-hundred-pound bulk, trying to bite me if I attempted to get past her. We engaged in a ridiculous game that involved me holding a spoonful of strawberries aloft, dancing from the kitchen into the garden like a pig Pied Piper, depositing the fruit into her open milky mouth, and running as fast as I could to lock the door behind me to the sound of porcine fury. In defeated distress, I called my aunt's assistant Sharon and explained the situation.

"Here's the thing," she said, in dulcet Zen tones. I took a deep breath and wondered what Doctor Dolittle trick she was going to impart, "It's very simple. Frances doesn't like change."

In the spirit of change, I give you the following. It's for leaf-sodden days and misty mornings.

Autumn
Breakfasts

Tapioca with stewed apples and apricots

Tapioca, like semolina, is one of those things that a school kitchen could have turned you off for life. I couldn't eat it for years, having been force-fed it at primary school aged six, with tinned jam, as it oozed like frogspawn out of the bowl and I wept and retched. For years I had the same malicious feeling toward beets and mashed potatoes, which were instant and came in lumpy granules. My teacher and I had a silent war every lunchtime; a war that eventually came to an end after my parents removed me from the school. Made to your own wont, in your own kitchen, tapioca is ambrosial, and worth being a grown-up for, as is semolina. This could also be a pudding, not a breakfast, just don't serve it with dog food–like tinned jam. Try a lovely homemade compote instead. *Pictured on page 8*.

Having soaked the tapioca overnight, drain and place it in a saucepan with the milk, vanilla extract, and butter. Bring to a boil, turn to low, and simmer, stirring in the honey, agave, or sugar, for another 10 minutes.

Cut your overnight magically plumped apricots into halves or quarters, if desired. In another saucepan, place the water, cinnamon, orange juice, agave or honey, and apples and bring to a boil, giving it a good stir now and then. Simmer for about 10 to 15 minutes, or until the apples are tender.

Now, here you can do one of two things. Serve the stewed fruit as is on top of the tapioca or put the tapioca in a small ovenproof dish with another tablespoon of butter, pour the apples and apricots on top, and bake at 350°F/180°C for 15 or so minutes. The choice, Cilla, is yours.

SERVES 4

½ cup/70 g tapioca (soaked overnight in plenty of water)

1⅓ cups/350 ml milk

1 teaspoon vanilla extract

1 tablespoon butter, plus more as needed

2 tablespoons runny honey, agave nectar, or brown sugar

For the apples and apricots

12 dried apricots (like the tapioca, soaked overnight, but in about 1 cup/250 ml orange juice)

1 cup/250 ml or so water

1 cinnamon stick

A few tablespoons of orange juice

1 tablespoon agave nectar or honey

2 eating apples, peeled, cored, and sliced

Argan oil, almond, and honey smoothie

SERVES 1

½ frozen peeled banana
8 or so blanched almonds
1 glass of soy milk
1 teaspoon Argan oil
1 tablespoon runny honey

Argan oil comes from the Argan tree, a Moroccan tree with magical properties. The oil is now easy to obtain through mail order or online, or if you live in a city, at your local health food shop. I get mine from Wild Wood Groves, www.wildwoodgroves.com. If you can't access it, use a cold-pressed oil instead, something like an almond oil. I eat Argan and put it on my face and in my bath. It's also great for babies with eczema. Frozen bananas are perfect for adding to smoothies, so have some in stock. Chop up the banana and put it in the freezer in a ziplock bag or plastic container.

Put your banana, almonds, soy milk, and Argan oil in the blender with your honey. Blend until smooth and drink and be joyful.

Crab cakes with poached eggs and spinach

Perhaps the thing I miss most about living in the United States is the ubiquity of brunch, or the ready availability of breakfast foods in a restaurant, long after breakfast is normally finished. Crab cakes are such a thing, perfectly so with eggs on top. If the mountain can't come to Mohammed ...

Get the crab cake mixture ready by mixing all the ingredients, bar the egg and olive oil, and forming into little cakes. Beat the egg and brush the crab cakes with it, then heat the olive oil in a nonstick frying pan. Throw on the crab cakes and cook them for a few minutes on each side until golden. You can also wilt the spinach in the same pan for a few minutes. Plate, with the spinach around the crab cakes.

In a saucepan, boil some water with a dash of vinegar and some salt. When it is simmering away, carefully crack in your eggs and poach for 3 minutes. Remove the eggs with a slotted spoon and put them on top of the crab cakes. Eat immediately.

SERVES 2

For the crab cakes
1 pound/450 g cooked
    crab meat
1 tablespoon homemade
    or good mayonnaise
1 teaspoon mustard
A few drops of Tabasco
    sauce
A small handful of
    chopped mixed fresh
    herbs—dill, chervil,
    and parsley
Salt and pepper
1 egg
2 tablespoons olive oil

A handful of spinach
A dash of vinegar
Salt
2 eggs

Spelt French toast with smashed blueberries and blackberries

SERVES 4

For the smashed blueberries and blackberries

2 generous handfuls each of blackberries and blueberries

1 tablespoon water

3 tablespoons agave nectar or honey

A day-old spelt loaf

4 eggs, plus 1 egg yolk

½ cup/125 ml milk

1 teaspoon vanilla extract

2 tablespoons agave nectar or brown sugar

Pinch of salt

1 tablespoon butter

4 heaping tablespoons Greek yogurt

Another very happy childhood food memory. French toast is as comforting as a feather-filled bed. *Pictured on pages 12–13.*

Put the berries in a saucepan with the water and agave or honey. Bring to a boil and simmer for a few minutes, or until the berries begin to split into a big, jammy autumnal mess.

Slice the stale loaf into manageable toast-sized pieces. In a mixing bowl, beat together the eggs and egg yolk with the milk, vanilla, agave or sugar, and salt. When well incorporated, pour this mixture into a shallow baking dish. Start putting the bread in it, making sure it's fully dunked. You need to let the bread sit in this eggy bath for at least 20 minutes, so it can really soak it up. If the bread needs help, prick it with a fork to help the egg mixture permeate.

Take a big griddle pan or large heavy-bottomed frying pan and melt the butter. Put the egg-soaked bread in, working in batches if need be. Cook it for about 4 minutes on each side, until the bread is bronzed on the outside and soft on the inside. Serve on warmed plates, with the smashed berries and yogurt on top.

Mushrooms
on toast

This is also perfect for a Sunday night supper when there are few around and you can eat this on your lap, a poached egg on top of it, watching a good old costume drama. *Pictured on pages 16–17.*

First of all, make sure your frying pan is searing hot. Otherwise, your mushrooms can get soggy and unpleasant and, frankly, a soggy mushroom is a bit grim. Toss in the mushrooms at the same time as the olive oil and the garlic. You should hear an angry hiss. Hurrah!

Keep throwing it all around and when the mushrooms are the burnished shade that appeals to you, toss in the parsley, tarragon, and butter. There should be lots of juices in the pan and I suggest you add to them with a drizzle of half-and-half. And maybe a splash of white wine? But I suppose it is breakfast. Season to taste and serve on crispy buttered toast with a big cup of tea.

SERVES 2

A good few handfuls of
  mixed wild mushrooms,
  coarsely chopped
1 tablespoon olive oil
1 clove garlic, peeled and
  finely chopped
A handful of chopped
  fresh parsley
A pinch of chopped fresh
  tarragon
1 tablespoon butter
A whisper of half-and-half
Salt and pepper
Slices of soda bread or
  dark rye, toasted and
  buttered

Apple cider omelet

SERVES 1

2 tablespoons butter

¼ small onion, peeled and finely chopped

2 teaspoons apple cider vinegar

Salt and pepper

3 eggs

½ cup/50 g grated sharp Cheddar cheese

1 teaspoon sumac

1 teaspoon chopped fresh thyme

There is nothing more English nor more autumnal than an apple swollen from the tree in late September. This omelet celebrates that in my house. Put your scarf on and kick some leaves!

Melt 1 tablespoon of the butter in a nonstick frying pan over medium heat. Add the onion and turn down the heat, cooking until it is soft. Add the apple cider vinegar and season, cooking until the vinegar is absorbed. Whisk the eggs in a small bowl, and, adding the rest of the butter to the frying pan, pour in the eggs over the onion mixture, making sure they're distributed evenly. Agitate them a bit and add the Cheddar, sumac, and thyme. Flip the omelet, cooking for another 30 seconds or so until cooked, and serve.

Gooseberry yogurt

Dedicated to my Aunt Lucy—a gooseberry fan. So much so that when she was in Amsterdam and saw gooseberries on the menu, she began shouting "Gooseberries!" at the top of her voice and did a little joyous dance, much to the amusement of my cousins, her daughters. She does live in Los Angeles, so is gooseberry deprived rather than just a bit weird.

Preheat the oven to 350°F/180°C. Put the gooseberries in an ovenproof baking dish and sprinkle with the sugar and orange flower water. Bake, uncovered, for about 20 minutes, take out, and leave to cool thoroughly. Strain the gooseberries, pour into the blender, and purée for a minute or so.

This can be eaten in a multitude of ways. Pour the gooseberry purée on top of the yogurt so it drips through, leave it on the bottom of the yogurt to find as a surprise, or ribbon it through.

SERVES 4

14 ounces/400 g gooseberries

2 tablespoons brown sugar

1 teaspoon orange flower water

¾ cup/185 ml Greek yogurt

Autumn
Lunches

Heartbreak carbonara
(or the first thing I ever cooked for a boy)

SERVES 4

4½ ounces/125 g pancetta,
    bacon, or ham
2 tablespoons olive oil
4 egg yolks
¼ cup/30 g grated
    Parmesan cheese
A splash of white wine
2 tablespoons light cream
Salt and pepper
18 ounces/500 g spaghetti

To marry with the wistful theme of my autumn, here is the first thing I ever cooked for a boy who I loved quietly and secretly. The carbonara in the pan lingered longer than he did—he wolfed it down with a bottle of Chianti, and informed me he was actually in love with a dancer called Willow (or something infinitely more exotic than Sophie). Then he disappeared into the night. I lay sobbing on the floor, wishing I could be angular and coordinated like Willow. Indeed, I cried such a ridiculous amount that in the morning I looked as if I had a black eye, and my mother gave me a heartbreak dispensation day off school.

Cut the pancetta into bite-sized pieces. In a medium-sized frying pan, warm the olive oil and cook the pancetta until crispy. Put to the side.

In a mixing bowl, beat together the egg yolks, Parmesan, splash of wine, the cream, and some salt and pepper. Add the pancetta and mix it all together. Cook the pasta and, as soon as it is ready, mix it quickly with the sauce so the egg doesn't cook.

Heartbreak not essential.

Squash and Parmesan soup

SERVES 4

4 tablespoons/50 g butter

2 pounds/1 kg squash, cubed

1 onion, peeled and finely chopped

1 clove garlic, peeled and finely chopped

2 tablespoons sherry

3½ cups/875 ml chicken or vegetable stock

½ teaspoon cayenne pepper

A couple of bay leaves

Salt and pepper

2 tablespoons heavy cream

A handful of toasted pumpkin seeds

A handful of chopped fresh parsley

A handful of grated Parmesan cheese

This is what blowsy October days are made for. Comforting and golden, this soup is a hymn to autumn. I first made this clucking around in upstate New York when I had some leftover squash. It works just as well with pumpkin or sweet potato.

In a heavy-bottomed saucepan, melt the butter and add the squash, onion, and garlic. Cook for a few minutes. Add the sherry, stir, and then add the stock, cayenne pepper, and bay leaves. Cook until the squash is tender, 10 to 15 minutes. Remove the bay leaves and blend the soup either with an immersion blender or in the blender. Season and add the cream. Serve with a topping of pumpkin seeds, parsley, and grated Parmesan.

Spanish omelet

Like a frittata, a bit of a recycling dish for what you've got lying around. Also great for a lunch box for a small or big person—just wrap in waxed paper.

Preheat the broiler to a high setting. In a large nonstick frying pan, heat 2 tablespoons of the oil on a medium to low flame. Add the potatoes and onions and cook until golden. Take off the heat and reserve.

Whisk the eggs in a large bowl and season them. Pour the onion and potato mix-ture into the eggs and heat the remaining tablespoon of olive oil in the pan. Add the egg mixture and turn down the heat to low. Loosen the edges and agitate the pan.

When the bottom is set and golden brown, take an oiled plate, turn the omelet out onto it, and put it back in the pan. Transfer the omelet to the hot broiler and cook for another minute or two until the top is set, then turn out, serving happily either hot or cold.

SERVES 4

3 tablespoons olive oil
1½ cups/225 g potatoes, peeled and thinly sliced
1⅓ cups/150 g onions, peeled and thinly sliced
8 eggs
Salt and pepper

BONFIRE NIGHT

I had been raiding the memory bank in order to come up with a recipe that captured all of the hissing November glory of Bonfire Night, but I first arrived at a feeling rather than a taste. Whether wrapped in the crisp skin of a twice-baked potato, or hidden amidst the charred sweetness of a sausage, rolling anticipation is the abiding sense of that night for me. Maybe it's a hangover from those teenage days— crushes seen through a wreath of bonfire smoke, against a backdrop of Technicolored sky, or the electric feel of cold fingers handing over an oozing marshmallow. Either way, the visuals are made flesh as soon as you eat something with a November tinge, from jaw-locking candy apples to mellow roasted pumpkin, and how . . .

"Fireworks in the heavens, fireworks in my head, one vodka too many, now I wish I was dead."

These were the words I wrote on the sixth of November, aged seventeen, nursing an aching head and heart. I had seen my love rat ex-boyfriend across a bonfire the night before and, oh woe, necked a couple of stiff vodkas and wobbled up to him, professing undying affection in the face of his horrible cheating ways. Love rat was a classic; twenty-seven to my seventeen, he'd disappear for nights on end and then eventually return with love bites and a bedraggled bouquet, probably nicked from a grave. He never had any money and was constantly dipping into my babysitting funds, and he only ever wore a black turtleneck, probably to hide the love bites.

On that night of sparklers, over the smell of chestnuts, he greeted my tear-thick protestations with fluttering eyelashes and a sly smile.

"Oh sweetheart, I've been away. Went to see a man about a dog in Leicester, you know how it is."

I didn't know how it was—how could I? I was green as a milk-fed calf, and I thought that if I just looked after him, made him lasagna, and kept him warm, he would love me as he had in August, and he might even stop drinking and disappearing. And after all, weren't the greatest love affairs meant to be a bit tortured in their onset? I was highly romantic and believed we were playing out a drama of old, I Caitlin to his Dylan, or he Burton to my Taylor.

As my friends rolled their eyes around the bonfire, he kissed me behind a bush, and then sloped home to his new girlfriend, a twenty-something Dane with stumpy legs, a BMW, and her own flat in Chelsea. I did not have a flat in Chelsea; I lived in Balham with my mum, had a curfew, and I couldn't drive.

"He doesn't really love her," I told my friend Cassie afterward, the relief of his kiss still reassuringly near. "He loves me. He told me, it was very sincere. I feel awful for him. He feels beholden to the Dane because she doesn't know anyone in London, and he's painting her flat. It's temporary. And anyway, I have better legs."

"Love," she said. "He's a total prat."

"Aren't they all?" I asked wearily, as the fireworks sang over my head. I felt that this was one of life's *moments*, one that I would remember always.

My association with the love rat lasted until Christmas, when the stumpy Dane who had stolen him from me called me crying. She read from my script, and I felt oddly sorry for her.

"He's gone missing," she said.

"He does that," I said. "It's horrible."

And as I said the things to her that everyone had said to me, it became real.

"You're worth more than this. Love is not meant to be about uncertainty. He's very lucky to have you."

The truth was liberating.

"He's a total arse," I told her. "I'd get rid of him if I were you."

It was November a good seven years later when I bumped into him. Red wine stained his teeth and gathered in the creases of his mouth. He looked like a vampire and stumbled with drink. He told me I was the great love of his life. I laughed. He still wore a turtleneck.

Baked pumpkin with lemon, sautéed greens, and toasted cumin dressing

This is perfect to serve with some quinoa or wild rice as a main to a non-meat eater, or as a side with some roast chicken for the carnivorous. It's also good served warm the following day with a little grilled tofu added. *Pictured on pages 30–31.*

Preheat the oven to 425°F/220°C. Put the pumpkin in a roasting pan with the onion and sage. Season and pour over the olive oil. Cook for around 30 minutes, or until the pumpkin is tender.

While the pumpkin is cooking, make your dressing. In a small frying pan on a medium heat, toast the cumin seeds. This should only take a minute, and you will know it's ready when the dusk of the cumin is wafting round your kitchen. Cool for a minute, then squeeze the lemon juice into the pan and add the olive oil. Put this into a pitcher or something and leave to the side, stirring in the crème fraîche just before serving.

Now, the greens. In a big frying pan, heat the olive oil and garlic. Throw in the greens and cook until tender, 5 to 10 minutes.

Take the pumpkin out of the oven. Put the greens on a plate, top with the pumpkin, and cover with the dressing.

SERVES 4

2 pounds/1 kg pumpkin, seeded and chopped into coarse slices
1 large red onion, peeled and coarsely sliced
A few fresh sage leaves, coarsely torn
Salt and pepper
2 tablespoons olive oil

For the dressing
1½ teaspoons cumin seeds or ground cumin
Juice of ½ lemon
1 tablespoon olive oil
1 teaspoon crème fraîche or sour cream

For the sautéed greens
2 tablespoons olive oil
1 clove garlic, peeled and finely chopped
A handful of Swiss chard
A handful of curly kale

Soba noodle salad with rainbow vegetables and sesame dressing

SERVES 2

9 ounces/250 g soba
   noodles

⅓ large daikon (about
   5 ounces/150 g), cut into
   thin strips

½ small head cabbage,
   shredded

1 medium carrot, peeled
   and grated

A handful of radishes,
   thinly sliced

1 green onion, finely
   shredded

1 small handful of sesame
   seeds

For the dressing

3 tablespoons sesame oil

1 tablespoon brown
   rice vinegar

1 teaspoon tamari
   (wheat-free soy sauce)

1 teaspoon agave nectar
   or honey

I put soba noodles in everything—soups, salads, and stir-fries. This is a quick, healthy, bountiful lunch and one to give to your friend who's allergic to *everything*.

Cook the soba noodles by bringing 8 cups/2 liters of water to a boil, adding the noodles, and cooking on low for 6 or so minutes. Drain and cool. When the noodles are cool, put them in the bowl you are planning to serve them in and add all of the vegetables—shredding, grating, and thinly slicing.

In a small frying pan, toast the sesame seeds for a minute or so. Add to the noodles. Make the dressing by whisking all the ingredients together, adjusting according to taste, and pour over the noodles.

Lentil salad with a mustard dressing

SERVES 4

1¼ cups/225 g Puy lentils

2 celery stalks, finely chopped

A handful of cherry tomatoes, finely chopped

1 cup/150 g crumbled feta cheese

A small handful of chopped fresh mint

For the dressing

¼ cup/60 ml olive oil or rapeseed oil

1 teaspoon white wine vinegar

2 teaspoons Dijon mustard

1 shallot, peeled and finely chopped

Salt and pepper

Lentils are always good things to have in stock, along with chickpeas. You can turn them into a salad or soup on the spot. This is a hearty salad that is also good warm. *Pictured on pages 34–35*.

Place the lentils in a saucepan and add just enough water to cover. Simmer over low heat for 20 minutes, then drain.

In a serving bowl, mix the lentils with the celery, tomatoes, and feta.

Make the dressing by whisking all the ingredients together, adjusting according to taste. Dress the salad and then toss with the mint.

Beef stroganoff

I know, I know. Totally from the same school as Chicken Kiev (page 165) in terms of 1980s nostalgia and naffness. But wasn't it good, particularly if it came in a ready meal? We knew not what we did. I used to beg for beef stroganoff as a child. I think, as a worthy vegetarian, it became Quorn stroganoff and now, somewhere in the middle, the last time I had anything resembling it was a mushroom variety in a pub in Cornwall. Good old retro food.

Put a frying pan over low heat and drop in the oil or butter. Add the onion and garlic and sweat for a few minutes, making sure they don't brown. Add the mushrooms and cook until they are golden. Put this mixture to the side.

In the same pan, heat a little more oil and add the beef strips, paprika, and lemon. Toss around. Cook for a minute or so, and then splash on the vermouth. Pour the mushroom and onion mixture back in the pan, cook for another minute but no longer, and then take off the heat and add the sour cream and the parsley. Mix it all together and serve with some simple boiled potatoes or rice.

SERVES 4

1 tablespoon olive oil or butter, plus extra oil
1 onion, peeled and finely chopped
1 clove garlic, peeled and finely chopped
2 handfuls of mushrooms, roughly chopped
18 ounces/500 g beef fillet, chopped into strips ½ inch/1 cm wide and thick
1 teaspoon paprika
Juice of ½ lemon
A splash of vermouth
¼ cup/60 ml sour cream
A handful of chopped fresh parsley

Autumn Suppers

Salmon fillets with a wasabi coating

I adore the kick that wasabi gives to anything in its path. Buy it in powder form and add *slowly* to dressings or mayonnaise, or if anyone you know goes to Japan, get them to bring you back some of the toxic green stuff in a tube. *Pictured on page 41.*

In a saucepan, cook the wild rice (two parts water to one part rice) by boiling for 45 minutes. Leave to the side to cool.

Meanwhile, in another saucepan, cover the beet with water; bring to a boil, then reduce the heat and simmer for about 30 minutes, until the beet is tender. Drain, and when cool enough to handle, peel off the skin and cut the beet into coarse chunks.

Chop the pomegranate in half and extract the seeds. Add the pomegranate, beet, olive oil, and mint to the rice. Leave to the side.

Make the wasabi coating by mixing together the mayonnaise, cumin, and wasabi. Taste and adjust if you want. Preheat the oven to 350°F/180°C.

Wash and dry the salmon, and season. Heat a griddle or ovenproof frying pan big enough to fit both salmon fillets and, when it is searing hot, drop in the salmon, skin-side down. Turn after 5 minutes or when the skin is brown and crispy. Take off the heat, carefully turn again, and spoon the wasabi coating onto the top of the salmon. Put the pan into the oven and cook for around 10 minutes, until the coating begins to brown. Serve on the wild rice.

SERVES 2

For the rice
¾ cup/100 g wild rice
1 large beet
1 pomegranate
1 tablespoon olive oil
A small handful of
    chopped fresh mint
Salt and pepper

For the wasabi coating
2 tablespoons mayonnaise
½ teaspoon ground cumin
1 teaspoon wasabi paste
    or powder mixed to
    a paste with water

2 salmon fillets, about
    6 ounces/175 g each
Salt and pepper

Baked eggplant smothered in scamorza

SERVES 2

1 large eggplant
Salt and pepper
2 tablespoons olive oil
1 ball smoked scamorza
 or smoked mozzarella
 cheese (or regular
 mozzarella)
Olive oil

For the pesto
1 large clove garlic, peeled
A large handful of fresh
 basil
A few tablespoons of pine
 nuts
3 tablespoons olive oil
¼ cup/30 g grated
 Parmesan cheese
Salt and pepper

Scamorza is an Italian cow's milk cheese, available in most Italian delis. If you can't find it, use mozzarella instead. The smoked scamorza lends a smoky depth to sauces and whatever it touches. It is also pretty bloody good on its own, eaten from the packet. This is a variation on a recipe given to me by my girlfriend Emma.

Preheat the oven to 350°F/180°C.

Start with salting the eggplant. Slice it lengthwise, put it on a kitchen towel, and sprinkle it with salt. Turn after 20 minutes or so, and do the other side. Rinse and dry thoroughly.

Make the pesto in a big mortar and pestle by grinding up the garlic. Add the basil, keep mashing away, and then add the pine nuts. Slowly add the olive oil, and then the Parmesan. Season to taste.

Put all the eggplant slices in an ovenproof dish and give them a good dash of olive oil. Bake for around 10 minutes. Take out of the oven and spread the pesto on the layer of eggplant, then add a layer of scamorza or mozzarella. Repeat the layering process until everything is used up. Bake for around 30 minutes and serve with a crisp green salad.

Root vegetable cakes with a cheesy béchamel sauce

You could serve this as an accompaniment to roast beef or any meat. Children seem to like these cakes, which are crispy outside and sweet and moreish on the inside. Serve with a gravy, either a meat-based one for the carnivores, or a mushroom or onion one for the non-meat eaters among us.

Add all of the vegetables *except* the spinach and leek to a saucepan of salted water and bring to a boil, cooking until soft. This should take about 15 minutes. Take the pan off the heat and drain the water, leaving about 1 inch, and mash the vegetables roughly with a tablespoon of butter and some salt and pepper.

In a small frying pan, heat the remaining tablespoon of butter and soften the spinach and leek for a few minutes. Mix the spinach and leek into the coarsely mashed vegetables and form the mixture into small cakes. Pop them in the fridge for an hour or so.

To make the sauce, put the milk in a saucepan with the carrot, onion, parsley, and peppercorns. Bring to a boil, turn down the heat, and simmer for 5 minutes. Strain out the vegetables and pour the milk into a measuring cup. Wash out the saucepan and dry, then melt the butter. Slowly add the arrowroot, stirring continuously. Very slowly add the milk, again stirring all the while. When it is incorporated and smooth, add the cheese and stir until it melts. Season to taste and if too thick, add a few more drops of milk.

In a big frying pan, heat the olive oil over medium heat. Put the cakes in and cook for a few minutes on each side, until they are lacy and golden. Serve with big spoonfuls of sauce.

SERVES 4

2 sweet potatoes, peeled and coarsely chopped

2 parsnips, peeled and coarsely chopped

2 carrots, peeled and coarsely chopped

A handful of chopped curly kale

½ celery root, peeled and chopped into small pieces

2 tablespoons butter

Salt and pepper

A handful of spinach, chopped

½ leek, cut into thin rounds

2 tablespoons olive oil

For the sauce

2 cups/500 ml milk

A few slices of carrot and onion

A few sprigs of fresh parsley

A few peppercorns

1 tablespoon butter

1 tablespoon arrowroot

½ cup/50 g grated sharp cheddar cheese

Salt and pepper

Tofu lasagna

SERVES 4

1 block/300 g firm tofu,
  drained, sliced ½ inch/
  1 cm thick, and patted
  dry with a kitchen towel

¼ cup/25 g finely grated
  Parmesan cheese

Salt and pepper

4 tablespoons olive oil,
  plus extra oil

4 portobello mushrooms,
  thickly sliced

7 ounces/200 g cherry
  tomatoes

2 cloves garlic, peeled and
  finely sliced

3 tablespoons balsamic
  vinegar

A handful of fresh basil,
  plus extra to garnish

8 to 12 fresh lasagna
  sheets

Something I used to make a lot on brisk nights when I lived in New York that, once again, even fussy children seem to like. If your carnivores are horrified by tofu, just substitute 14 ounces/400 g coarsely ground beef and brown it in a very hot pan with the olive oil. Instead of leaving to one side, carry on cooking with the sauce, and assemble as you would the original.

Coat the tofu in the Parmesan cheese, season generously, and fry the slices in 2 tablespoons of the oil until brown. Set aside. Fry the mushrooms in the remaining oil until browned, add the tomatoes and garlic, and fry until the tomatoes are bursting. Add the balsamic and bubble down to caramelize. Throw in a splash of water along with the basil leaves to make a sauce. Stir and remove from the heat. Season with salt and pepper.

Cook the pasta according to the package instructions. Drain in a colander and toss in a drizzle of olive oil to prevent the sheets sticking to each other. When just cool enough to handle, layer the pasta, tofu, and mushroom mixture up on each plate, finishing with a couple of spoonfuls of the pan sauce and fresh basil leaves.

Chickpea-mushroom burgers with tahini sauce

SERVES 4

2 tablespoons olive oil, plus extra for frying

1 onion, peeled and finely chopped

2 cloves garlic, peeled and finely chopped

18 ounces/500 g cooked and drained chickpeas

A handful of wild mushrooms, coarsely torn

2 teaspoons ground cumin

2 teaspoons ground coriander

A small handful of chopped fresh parsley

3 tablespoons spelt or all-purpose flour

Salt and pepper

Hearty, and not at all pious feeling, these are an easy thing to pull together if you have little time. Woodsy and delicious, they would also be good for a BBQ. *Pictured on pages 50–51.*

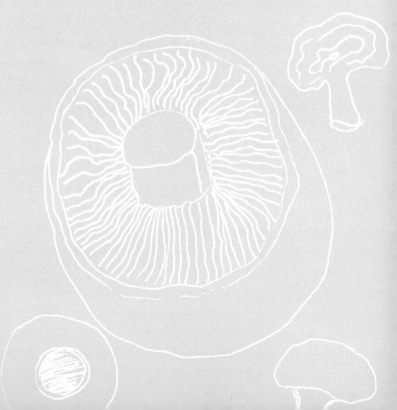

Heat a frying pan and pour in the olive oil. Add the onion and garlic and sweat for a few minutes.

Put all of the other ingredients in a blender or food processor and add the softened onion-garlic mixture. Pulse until you have the consistency of bread crumbs. Take out the mixture and fashion it into burgers.

Heat a tablespoon or two of olive oil in a frying pan and cook the burgers for a few minutes on each side, until crispy and golden brown.

Mix the tahini sauce ingredients in a bowl and pour on top of the burgers. Eat with some minted rice or on buns!

For the tahini sauce
3 tablespoons olive oil
1 tablespoon tahini
Juice of ½ lemon

Lentil pie

You can leave this bare, top with a celery root–rutabaga mash or colcannon, smother in cheese, or serve alongside rice. Whatever you do, eat it piping hot, with lots of peas on the side, and possibly some ketchup.

Place the lentils in a saucepan and add just enough water to cover. Simmer over low heat for 20 minutes, then drain.

In a large frying pan, heat the olive oil. Throw in the onion and garlic and cook over low heat until soft. Add the carrots and cook for a few minutes. Add the tomatoes and celery, followed by the red wine, then the stock, Worcestershire sauce, Tabasco, and bay leaves. Stir all the while. Add the balsamic vinegar and the parsley. Let cook for another few minutes, and then add the lentils. Cook for a few minutes and serve in bowls, with a dollop of crème fraîche or sour cream, some more parsley, or perhaps some spinach.

SERVES 4

½ cup/100 g Puy lentils

2 tablespoons olive oil

1 large red onion, peeled and finely chopped

2 cloves garlic, peeled and crushed

2 large carrots, peeled and chopped quite small

1 cup/200 g canned plum tomatoes

2 celery stalks, chopped

1 small glass of red wine

2½ cups/600 ml vegetable stock

1 tablespoon Worcestershire sauce, or to taste

A few drops of Tabasco sauce

A few bay leaves

1 teaspoon syrupy balsamic vinegar

A small handful of chopped fresh parsley, plus extra to garnish

Crème fraîche or sour cream, to taste

The first Mor Mor and her chicken

My great-grandmother, a Norwegian, Sofie Magdalene Hesselberg, was known as the first Mor Mor in my family. "Mor Mor" is an affectionate moniker used by grandchildren in many Scandinavian countries, referring to their "mother's mother."

Sofie was a tough cookie. Having emigrated in her early twenties from Norway to Wales, she lost her husband and eldest daughter within a few months of each other, and was left in a foreign country with three small children of her own and two stepchildren to take care of. A lesser woman would have been felled. Mor Mor got on with it, fulfilling her late husband's wishes of putting all his children through the British school system, and managing to keep a staunch sense of humor and practicality during what must have been a shattering time. She told her children Norse legends about trolls, fjord-dwelling spirits, and fairies. She also smoked cigars and had a crystal ball. I wish I had known her.

One of her daughters remembers Mor Mor making the following during the war, when they lived near a farmer who would sometimes donate to them a chicken on the sly. It has been passed down, and here it is.

Place the chicken in a large casserole and pour the chicken stock over it until it is nearly covered. Add a quarter of the carrots, all of the onions, the bouquet garni, and bay leaf and bring to a boil. When it has boiled, turn it down and simmer over very low heat for 2 hours. About 1 hour and 40 minutes in, add the remaining carrots and all the potatoes, and top up with more stock if need be. About 3 minutes before the 2 hour mark, add the peas.

Take the chicken and vegetables out of the casserole and leave to the side. Take the remaining juices in the casserole and strain as a stock for the sauce.

Melt the butter in a saucepan, gently add the flour, and cook over low heat for a few minutes. Add the stock, bit by bit, stirring continuously. Season to taste, and then start gently adding the milk. Cook for several minutes.

Hopefully your chicken will be cool enough to touch. Remove all the flesh from the carcass and get rid of the skin. Put the chicken and vegetables back in the casserole, cover with the sauce, and heat gently. Serve with some parsley.

SERVES 4 TO 6

1 medium-sized happy
   free-range chicken
5 cups/1.2 liters chicken
   stock
1½ pounds/700 g carrots,
   peeled and cut into
   coarse chunks
2 medium onions, peeled
   and finely sliced
A bouquet garni
1 bay leaf
7 ounces/200 g potatoes,
   cut into coarse chunks
1½ cups/225 g frozen peas
4 tablespoons/50 g butter
Scant ½ cup/50 g
   all-purpose flour
Salt and pepper
1¼ cups/300 ml milk
A handful of chopped
   fresh parsley

Vine Tomatoes

Winter

WINTER BREAKFASTS AND DANCING PIGEONS

Among the many odd things I have done, none was odder than my turn, many years ago, as a leading lady in a Bollywood film. I was unspeakably bad in it and it cured me of any latent desire to be an actress. I should also think it cured anyone watching of the desire to ever see me act again. However, I can lip synch in Hindi while dancing with bells on my ankles, which may one day come in handy.

I am not a natural synchronized dancer. I am incredibly graceless and can't follow instructions. I remember being struck dumb with terror and embarrassment as a bevy of Bollywood lovelies, backing dancers, stood behind me, rolling their eyes as I tried to pick up some simple step. The terror was exacerbated one day when I came to work to dance barefoot and was confronted by a very large rustling crate that seemed to coo and scratch and breathe.

"What is in that crate?" I asked.

"Oh, it's the dancing pigeons," the director replied, breezily. "Five hundred of them. They will dance around your feet, while you dance. It will be one big happy dance party. Yeah!"

Reader, I hate pigeons. I loathe and abhor them. I hate them in the sky, but I hate them more if they are "dancing" with their scabby, prehistoric feet, next to my own clumsy, enormous, BARE feet in an echoing sound stage in Mumbai.

"Are you bloody joking?" I said with mounting panic. "You want me to dance barefoot in the midst of five hundred pigeons?! And look like a joyful village belle?"

"Yes," the director said, with a steely look, one I could not face arguing with.

I "danced" with a veil in the middle of a sea of five hundred pigeons. There is a look of maniacal fear on my face, as I navigated around pigeon droppings and small claws, remembering to lip synch in Hindi and not count time out loud. I think it took about ten hours, although it felt like a lifetime. Those bastard pigeons didn't make the final cut.

Having spent a few solitary months in Mumbai, I also became particularly partial to an Indian breakfast. I was very lonely, and it was the highlight of my day. I made friends with the room service waiter, Akesh, who every morning seemed disappointed that I had not morphed into the screen siren Aishwarya Rai overnight. His eyes fell when he saw it was still dreary me in my pajamas, a Bollywood pretender. So to him I apologize, but to you I say, dosa recipes are far more useful than tinkling ankles and making friends with pigeons.

Winter
Breakfasts

Dosa

SERVES 4 TO 6

½ cup/90 g rice flour

½ cup/60 g semolina

¼ cup/60 ml whole milk
   plain yogurt

A handful of chopped
   fresh cilantro

1 cup/250 ml water

2 tablespoons sunflower
   oil or ghee

An easy yogurt dosa batter for an Indian breakfast with aloo gobi (facing page) and chutney. *Pictured on pages 64–65.*

In a large mixing bowl, mix the flour and semolina with the yogurt, cilantro, and water. Cover the bowl and leave on the side for a few hours. You may need to add a few spoonfuls of water just before cooking, as the flour will thicken and suck up all the liquid in sight! You want a thin batter consistency, but not so thin that it sticks to the pan.

Heat a nonstick griddle and brush with the oil or ghee. Make one test dosa by pouring a ladleful of batter into the pan, trying to keep it as evenly dispersed and thin as possible. When it is bubbling and pinpricked, turn it and cook the other side for a minute or two. Hopefully you've found your formula and the rest will be a breeze. Serve immediately with aloo gobi and some chutney.

Aloo gobi

Heat the oil or ghee in a heavy-bottomed saucepan. Add the chopped onion and cook on a medium heat until softened. Add the spices, chile, and curry leaves and mix together, cooking for a few minutes. Next, add the tomatoes and potatoes with the water and bring to a boil. Reduce the heat slightly and let cook on low for 10 to 15 minutes. Add the cauliflower, sugar, lemon juice, and cinnamon. Stir it all in, adding a little more water if the mixture is looking dry, and cook for another 10 to 15 minutes. Season to taste.

This is even more delicious the next day, after a night in the fridge, liberally covered in chopped cilantro. *Pictured on pages 64–65.*

SERVES 3 OR 4

2 tablespoons sunflower oil or ghee
1 small onion, peeled and finely chopped
½ teaspoon ground coriander
½ teaspoon ground turmeric
½ teaspoon ground ginger
1 teaspoon mustard seeds
1 small green chile, seeded (or not, according to your heat tolerance) and finely chopped
A few curry leaves
1 cup/250 g chopped tomatoes (fresh or canned)
4 medium potatoes, peeled and quartered
About 6 tablespoons water
½ small head of cauliflower, broken up into florets
½ teaspoon sugar
1 teaspoon lemon juice
A pinch of ground cinnamon
Salt and pepper

Soda bread with goat cheese and blistered tomatoes

SERVES 2

For the soda bread

3 cups/400 g stone-ground whole wheat flour or all-purpose flour (I've also used spelt flour and that works, too)

1 teaspoon baking soda

1 teaspoon salt

1⅓ cups/350 ml buttermilk

Soda bread is so easy, and discovering the ease of it makes the world of bread making suddenly seem far less frightening and more accessible. This is a gorgeous wintry breakfast, made better still with a bit of olive oil and a pinch of sea salt. *Pictured on pages 68–69.*

Preheat the oven to 400°F/200°C.

In a large mixing bowl, mix together the dry ingredients and make a well in the center of the bowl with your hand. Pour all of the buttermilk into the well and, using your hand, mix the flour into the buttermilk in a circular motion, from the well to the sides, so you draw all the flour into the middle. You want the dough soft, but not too sticky or elastic. This shouldn't take long and you don't want to meddle around with the dough too much. Put the dough onto a floured surface or board.

Give the dough a gentle roll with your hands to shape it into a ball and turn it over. Place it on a floured baking sheet, cut a deep cross in the middle, and put it in the oven. Bake for 40 minutes. If you're not sure if it's ready, tap the base, which should sound hollow.

To make the blistered tomatoes, preheat the broiler to very hot. Wash and dry the tomatoes, taking care to keep their vine intact. Set them in a roasting pan, season, pour on a glug of both the olive oil and balsamic vinegar, and then sprinkle with the thyme. Broil for 5 to 10 minutes or until the skins are just beginning to break and char.

Smear your bread with goat cheese, curl your tomatoes up by it, and spoil it all by mashing them into the cheesy bread and eating. Yum.

For the blistered tomatoes

12 to 16 small tomatoes on the vine

Salt and pepper

A glug of olive oil

A glug of good, thick balsamic vinegar (I use white balsamic, but any will do)

A tablespoon or so of chopped fresh thyme

½ cup/50 g soft goat cheese

Mexican eggs

SERVES 2

1 tablespoon butter or
  olive oil
½ onion, peeled and finely
  chopped
2 tomatoes, finely chopped
1 small green chile, seeded
  and finely chopped
4 eggs
½ cup/50 g queso fresco
  (crumbly Mexican
  cheese) or grated
  Manchego cheese
Salt and pepper
A small handful of finely
  chopped fresh cilantro

Who cares if we're stuck in England in December? We have these eggs to remind us of the faraway, and they're a lot cheaper than a return flight to Cabo. Serve with some spicy hot chocolate. (Add a cinnamon stick and a pinch of chile powder to your hot chocolate pan and leave to infuse over low heat for a few minutes.)

On a lowish heat, melt the butter or oil in a heavy-bottomed frying pan. Add the onion and cook for a few minutes, and then add the tomatoes and chile and give a good stir. While these are cooking, whisk the eggs into the mixture, stirring gently all the time as you would with scrambled eggs.

Add the cheese at the last moment, season to taste, and serve sprinkled liberally with cilantro unless you are my brother-in-law, Ben Cullum, who has a mortal loathing of the stuff. I like these eggs smothered with Tabasco sauce with a bowl of guacamole on the side.

Porridge with poached plums

I could quite happily eat porridge every day. Cold, too, with honey. I could be hired as the fourth bear.

Soak the oats overnight in 1 cup/250 ml of the water. Leave to the side, covered with a kitchen towel. When you wake up, pour the oats into a saucepan and bring to a boil with the remaining 2 cups/500 ml of water. When you have it at a rolling boil, turn down the heat, add a pinch of salt, and simmer on low for around 45 minutes.

While your porridge is cooking, make the poached plums. Put the plums in a saucepan, cover with the water, and add the agave or sugar and the spices. Bring to a boil and then simmer until the fruit is soft, about 5 or so minutes.

Serve the porridge with a generous tablespoon of the plums and their juice. If you want to be very decadent, add a lick of cream.

SERVES 4

1 cup/100 g steel-cut oats
   (like McCann's)
3 cups/750 ml water
A pinch of salt

For the plums
1 pound/450 g plums,
   pitted and quartered
1½ cups/375 ml water
4 tablespoons agave
   nectar or brown sugar
1 cinnamon stick
A few cloves

Warming winter take on miso soup

SERVES 2

- 1½ cups/400 ml vegetable stock
- 1 carrot, peeled and coarsely grated
- 4 shiitake mushrooms, stemmed and sliced
- 1 parsnip, peeled and coarsely grated
- ½ onion, peeled and thinly sliced in half-moon shapes
- ½ block/150 g firm tofu, drained and patted dry with a kitchen towel
- 1 tablespoon sesame oil
- 1 to 2 tablespoons barley miso paste (most health food shops stock this)
- 1 green onion, finely chopped

Earthy miso soup, another breakfast friend discovered during my weird nomadic former career. Of course it should be served at breakfast time—try it and see. It makes total sense. I would have this with a little bowl of rice and some pickles. *Pictured on page 72.*

In a medium-sized saucepan, pour in the stock and add the grated carrot, mushrooms, parsnip, and onion and bring to a boil. Reduce the heat and cook on low for 15 to 20 minutes.

Cut the tofu into small cubes and, in a separate frying pan, heat the oil over medium-high heat and cook the tofu until it is golden brown. Drain the oil and add the tofu to the soup. Mix the miso paste with a couple of spoonfuls of the soup and pour it into the saucepan. Give the soup a good stir. Add the chopped green onion and serve.

Poached pears with healthy vanilla custard

Obviously custard is good made with ladles of cream and sugar, this we know. But at breakfast time, a river of heavy cream custard may be pushing it and your blood sugar levels. This way, my friends, is perfectly respectable and still delicious.

Make sure you have a shallow pan that all your pears will fit in. Put the apple juice, agave or honey, cinnamon stick, and star anise into the pan and bring to a boil, stirring to incorporate the agave. When bubbling, turn down the heat, add the pears, and cook over low to medium heat for about 10 minutes. When the pears are soft, turn off the heat and leave to the side.

For the custard, pour the milk into a saucepan and scrape the insides of the vanilla bean into it. Heat the milk until it begins to bubble, and then take it off the heat. In a mixing bowl, whisk together the egg yolks, arrowroot, and the maple syrup or agave nectar, and, when combined, slowly whisk in the warm milk. Strain the custard into a clean pan and heat on low, whisking until the custard is thick and warm. Serve right away on top of the pears.

SERVES 4

For the pears
2 cups/500 ml apple juice
¼ cup/60 ml agave nectar
  or honey
1 cinnamon stick
1 star anise
4 pears, peeled, cored, and
  halved

For the custard
1¼ cups/300 ml low-fat
  milk
1 vanilla bean, slit in half
2 egg yolks
2 teaspoons arrowroot
¼ cup/60 ml maple syrup
  or agave nectar

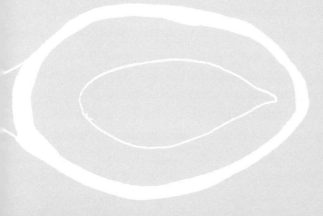

Winter
Lunches

Cauliflower chowder and a brilliant bread recipe

For the bread

A small handful each of poppy seeds, sunflower seeds, and pumpkin seeds

3 cups/450 g whole wheat flour

1 cup/115 g spelt flour

2 tablespoons brown sugar

1 teaspoon or a large pinch of salt

1 egg

2 cups/500 ml plain yogurt

1 tablespoon olive oil

On the twisting road halfway between San Francisco and Big Sur in lashing rain, my friend and I came across a farm stand, like a mirage. There was cauliflower chowder on a hot plate, homemade bread and butter, chocolate chip cookies, and beautiful peaches. There was no one serving, you put your money in a glass jar. We sat in contented silence, our soup in paper cups, bread in our hands, thanking the day we were born. This is an ode to that day.

Grease a loaf pan and sprinkle the inside with an even coating of poppy seeds. Mix together the flours, sugar, and salt in a big mixing bowl. Separately, mix the egg, yogurt, and olive oil in a large measuring cup (or something similar). Gradually add the wet to the dry, mixing well. Your dough should feel sticky and damp. Sprinkle the other seeds over the dough. Place the dough in the prepared loaf pan and leave it in a warm place, covered with a kitchen towel, for 2 hours.

Preheat the oven to 350°F/180°C. Bake the loaf for 1 hour or so, and then take it out and check that it makes a hollow sound when you tip it out of the loaf pan and tap the base. Place on a wire rack to cool.

For the soup, heat the olive oil or butter in a big, heavy-bottomed saucepan over low to medium heat. Add the onion, potatoes, and celery and cook for a few minutes. Pour in the chicken stock and half of the milk.

Add the cauliflower and flake the haddock into the soup, topping up with milk if needed. Simmer for about 15 minutes, slowly adding the rest of the milk. Add the half-and-half shortly before you serve. Season with salt and pepper and give it a generous handful of parsley. Serve with the bread.

For the chowder
1 tablespoon olive oil or
  butter
1 onion, peeled and finely
  chopped
2 potatoes, diced
2 celery stalks, finely diced
2½ cups/600 ml chicken
  stock (preferably fresh
  free-range chicken stock)
1 cup/250 ml milk
1 small head cauliflower,
  broken up into small
  florets
1 large smoked haddock
  fillet
3 tablespoons half-and-
  half
Salt and pepper
A handful of chopped
  fresh parsley

Taleggio gratin

You can play around with this using different types of vegetables, but avoid anything that gets too watery or the gratin becomes a running mess. Do drain the spinach properly and squash all the excess water out.

Start with the sauce. Melt the butter in a saucepan over medium heat and whisk in the flour. Pour in the milk, whisking constantly, and cook until it starts to boil. Season, decrease the heat, and simmer on low for about 10 minutes. Remove from the heat and taste, adding a pinch of nutmeg, if you like it. Add more milk if the sauce is too thick.

Sprinkle the celery root with a little salt to season. Put half the butter in a large saucepan, add the celery root, and cook over medium heat for 5 or so minutes, stirring. Add a tablespoon of water, cover the pan, and cook the celery root until tender, about 15 minutes.

In a small saucepan, heat the olive oil and add the onion, cooking on low for 10 minutes, or until soft. Add the spinach, season, and cook for another 3 minutes or so to wilt. Drain.

Preheat the oven to 400°F/200°C and grease an ovenproof dish with 1½ teaspoons of olive oil.

Put a layer of the celery root slices into your ovenproof dish and cover with the spinach and onion and then a layer of béchamel. Sprinkle some Taleggio on top. Carry on this process in layers until all of your ingredients are used up, ending with a layer of cheese-sprinkled béchamel. Bake for 20 minutes, or until golden and bubbling.

SERVES 4

For the béchamel sauce
4 tablespoons butter
⅓ cup/40 g all-purpose flour
2½ cups/580 ml milk
Salt and pepper
A pinch of freshly grated nutmeg (optional)

For the gratin
4 celery roots (about 4½ pounds/2 kg), peeled, halved, and thinly sliced
Salt and pepper
3 tablespoons butter
2 tablespoons olive oil, plus extra to grease the dish
1 small onion, peeled and thinly sliced
1 pound/450 g spinach, coarsely chopped
½ cup/60 g sliced Taleggio cheese

Stuffed blini and scrambled eggs

I made this on New Year's Eve for a few people in my kitchen. It's that perfect combination of treat and comfort and it works as a weekend breakfast, lunch, or dinner. You can use any cheese or herb combination that takes your fancy—Cheddar and chive with a bit of mustard powder is also good, as is Parmesan with some very thinly sliced sun-dried tomatoes chucked in. Even though it is simple, it feels a ceremony.

Into a large mixing bowl, sift together the flour, baking powder, and salt. Add the milk and whisk well to make a batter. Add the ricotta, chives, and parsley and mix again. In a separate clean bowl, whisk the egg whites until they form soft peaks. Fold them gently into the batter, being careful not to overmix.

In a small frying pan (preferably nonstick), heat a little butter or olive oil and spoon in a ladleful of the batter to cover the pan. Cook for 3 to 4 minutes until pinprick bubbles appear and you can easily turn the blini. Cook the other side for a minute or so, then remove the blini from the pan. Continue until all the batter is used up. If you are a great multitasker, you can make the scrambled eggs at the same time. If not, pop the blini in a warm oven while you're making the eggs.

To make the scrambled eggs, whisk the eggs and egg yolks and season. In a medium-sized frying pan, heat the butter over low heat. Add the eggs, stirring continuously and adding a little milk if they are dry. After a minute or so, take off the heat and continue to stir as the eggs will cook themselves. Put a blini (or two) on each plate and serve covered in scrambled eggs and chopped herbs.

SERVES 4

For the blini
1½ cups/175 g buckwheat flour
2 teaspoons baking powder
A pinch of salt
1¼ cups/300 ml milk
½ cup/150 g ricotta cheese
A small handful of finely chopped fresh chives and parsley, plus extra to garnish
4 egg whites (use the yolks for the scrambled eggs)
A tablespoon of butter or spoonful of olive oil

For the scrambled eggs
2 eggs
4 egg yolks
Salt and pepper
1 tablespoon butter
A dash of milk (optional)

Salad of brown rice and pearl barley with cranberries

SERVES 6 TO 8

2 tablespoons olive oil

1 small onion, peeled and finely chopped

1 cup/200 g brown rice, rinsed

1 cup/200 g pearl barley, rinsed

4 cups/1 liter water

A pinch of salt

½ red cabbage, finely shredded

1 celery stalk, finely diced

A handful of dried cranberries

A handful of chopped fresh parsley

A handful of pecans

For the dressing

1 tablespoon red wine vinegar

3 tablespoons olive oil

1 shallot, peeled and finely chopped

A big pinch of finely chopped fresh thyme

Salt and pepper

A colorful salad filled with goodness and complex aminos. Dried cranberries are marvelous and are readily available in most supermarkets and health food shops. You could add some toasted walnuts or almonds to this. You could also swap a grain for another: red rice, couscous, the possibilities are many.

In a large saucepan, heat the olive oil. Add the onion and sweat for a few minutes, and then stir in the grains. Add the water and salt and bring to a boil. When boiling, reduce the heat and simmer over low heat for 30 to 40 minutes. Leave to the side to cool.

When the grains have cooled, transfer them to a salad bowl and add the shredded cabbage, celery, cranberries, and parsley. Toast the pecans in a small frying pan for a few minutes and add to the salad.

Mix the dressing ingredients in a bowl and pour over the salad. Serve.

Watercress and Gruyère soufflés

The mere mention of the word "soufflé" has historically been enough to strike fear into the hearts of those who are ordinarily hardy in the kitchen. In the face of that golden mountain of unpredictability, many are rendered quivering wrecks. The soufflé is the bad boy of the kitchen, the one whose negative traits are legend. This character, which others warn us about, is unstable and liable to burn us. It's reputation seems a bit unfair—a vulnerable artistic type, yes, but in the flesh, oh how rewarding, complex, and delicious.

I'll give you a case in point for the defense. A thirteen-year-old me, bored, on a rainy Saturday, finding a soufflé recipe in an old cookbook of my mum's. We had eggs, flour, cheese, and butter in the house, so I thought I'd give it a go. Nobody was there to shake a head, or tell me how difficult it was going to be. So I made one. It came out of the oven, high and beautiful, a perfect illustration of the heady alchemy that goes on in cooking. My mum came home from the shops, or tarot card reader, or wherever she was, and was shocked to the core.

"You made a soufflé!" she cried.

"Yeah." I said. "So?"

Cut to years later, a twenty-one-year-old me, poisoned by years of meddling warnings from cookery shows and books, cooking a soufflé for a boyfriend (and six friends) who I was showing off to. It came out of the

(continued)

SERVES 6

2 tablespoons butter, plus
softened butter to coat
the ramekins

2 cups/230 g grated
Gruyère cheese

1 small bunch (2 ounces/
50 g) of watercress,
tough stalks removed

¼ cup/30 g all-purpose
flour

1¼ cups/300 ml low-fat
milk

6 eggs, separated

Salt and pepper

A pinch of nutmeg

oven a flat, miserable, eggy mess, which reduced my boasting and me to shreds.

The moral of the story is, don't be swayed by other people's experience. Experiment with the coolness of a child.

Preheat the oven to 400°F/200°C. Grease six 1-cup/250-ml ramekins with the softened butter and then coat with ¼ cup/30 g of the cheese. Place the ramekins on a baking sheet and chill in the fridge.

Blanch the watercress quickly in a saucepan of boiling water, remove immediately, and plunge into ice water, and then squeeze out all of the water. Stick the watercress in the blender and purée or chop very finely, then leave it on the side.

Melt the rest of the butter in a saucepan over low heat and add the flour to make a roux, stirring continuously for about a minute. Add the milk bit by bit, still stirring constantly. Let the sauce bubble for a minute or two and add the remaining cheese. Continue stirring until all the cheese has melted. Remove from the heat and leave to cool for a few minutes, then stir in the egg yolks and season, adding at this point the puréed watercress and the nutmeg.

In a separate very clean bowl, whisk the egg whites and a pinch of salt until they form stiff peaks. Gently fold half of the whites into the cheese-watercress sauce until combined, taking care not to over-mix, as you want to keep the mixture airy. Fold in the other half of the egg whites.

Divide the mixture evenly among the ramekins and level the tops with a spatula. Run the tip of your thumb around the inside of each dish to make a gap between the soufflé and the rim, which will help the soufflé to rise. Leave the ramekins on the baking sheet and bake for at least 15 minutes, possibly longer. *Don't* open the oven to check—resist the urge, however great. If the door is opened, the soufflés will collapse. When the soufflés are golden and majestic, serve immediately and, if they should collapse, you must not. Laugh instead.

Belgian endive salad with poached duck eggs and truffle vinaigrette

Duck eggs are rich, gamy, and largely unsung. They poach beautifully and, paired with the crisp Belgian endive and earthy truffle, they are total bliss. My mum used to fry them for breakfast.

Wash and trim the ends off the endives, separating the leaves. Dry and lay the leaves on four plates. In a small frying pan, toast the walnuts over medium heat for a few minutes.

Make the dressing by whisking together the truffle oil, shallot, vinegar, lemon juice, and salt and pepper. Adjust to taste.

Bring some water to a simmer in a saucepan with a splash of vinegar and some salt. Carefully crack in the duck eggs and poach for 3 minutes. Remove the eggs with a slotted spoon and put on top of the endives, with a sprinkling of walnuts and the dressing spooned on.

SERVES 4

4 Belgian endives
1 handful of walnuts, chopped
A splash of white wine vinegar
Salt
4 duck eggs

For the dressing
2 tablespoons truffle oil
½ shallot, peeled and finely chopped
1¼ teaspoons champagne vinegar or white wine vinegar
A quick squeeze of lemon juice
Salt and pepper

Quiche with crispy Canadian bacon and caramelized onions

SERVES 4 TO 6

For the pastry
2½ cups/275 g white spelt
   flour or all-purpose flour
½ teaspoon salt
1 cup/200 g butter
2 eggs, separated
3 tablespoons water

The pastry of this lovely quiche comes courtesy of Callie Hope-Moreley, and it is a proper French *pâte brisée* (French butter pastry), except I have made it with spelt flour. Oh, for a quiche that puffs up and trembles when it comes out of the oven. I hate those solid lumps of pastry, with solid lumps of egg. I want quivering Cartland heroines in my quiche. As long as they are not pink. I feel like the bacon keeps this sturdy. *Pictured on page 91.*

Sift the flour and salt into the bowl of a food processor fitted with the metal blade. Cut the butter into small cubes and add it to the flour. Whiz up the mixture until it resembles fine bread crumbs. Keeping it on, add the egg yolks and a few spoons of water to mix the dough. Take out the dough and lightly knead into a ball. Wrap in plastic wrap and place in the fridge for about half an hour. Preheat the oven to 400°F/200°C.

Grease a deep 11-inch/28-cm quiche pan and roll out the dough thinly. Line the dish with the pastry, removing any air pockets. Prick the base with a fork and bake blind for 20 minutes. Remove the pastry and keep to the side. Turn the oven up to 450°F/230°C.

While the pastry is baking, caramelize the onion. In a heavy-bottomed frying pan, heat a glug of olive oil and add the onion, stirring and stirring and making sure it is covered in the oil. You want to do this over low heat as the goal is for the onion to become golden, not charred. A heat diffuser can help. This will take about 20 minutes. Keep the onion to the side.

In a saucepan, melt the butter and add the flour to make a roux. Add the milk, bit by bit, stirring slowly and continuously until thick and just simmering. Simmer for a few minutes, then add the cheese and stir until melted. Take off the heat and add the bacon, mustard powder, salt and pepper, and the caramelized onion. In a separate bowl, whip the egg whites until they form stiff peaks, and gently fold them into the lovely roux. Pour it all into the pastry and bake for 25 to 30 minutes. Serve immediately.

For the filling

A glug of olive oil

1 large onion, peeled and finely chopped

6 tablespoons/75 g butter

¾ cup/75 g white spelt flour

2½ cups/570 ml low-fat milk

1 cup/110 g grated Cheddar cheese

8 ounces/225 g Canadian bacon, chopped, fried, and crispy

A pinch of mustard powder

Salt and pepper

Winter Suppers

Winter curry with saffron-cinnamon rice

SERVES 4 TO 6

For the garam masala
1 teaspoon cumin seeds
1 teaspoon mustard seeds
½ teaspoon cloves
1 teaspoon ground
   turmeric
6 cardamom pods, seeds
   only

*For the saffron-
cinnamon rice*
1½ cups/300 g basmati rice
1¾ cups/450 ml water
1 tablespoon butter
A couple of cardamom
   pods
A pinch of saffron
2 cinnamon sticks

This is sweet and filled with flavor, and you can tailor your garam masala to your own tastes, adjusting as you like. The rice is pretty foolproof, the method taught to me by Peter Begg, a man who knows about food. *Pictured on page 99.*

In a mortar and pestle, make the garam masala by crushing up and grinding all your dry spices.

To make the saffron-cinnamon rice, put the rice in a sieve and rinse until the water runs clear. Put the rice in a large saucepan with the water, butter, cardamom, saffron, and cinnamon. Bring to a rolling boil, quickly turn the heat down, put a lid on the saucepan, and simmer for 10 minutes. Remove the lid and take it to the table in the saucepan, because it looks like a painting.

In a heavy-bottomed casserole or pan, heat the safflower oil and add the onions, sweating over low heat until soft and translucent. Add the garlic and stir for another half a minute, taking care not to burn It. Add to this mix the garam masala and the chile and coat the onions with the spices. Add the pumpkin and chickpeas and then pour over the stock, followed by the coconut milk. Season and simmer for 10 to 15 minutes, add the snow peas, and cook for another 5 minutes.

Serve the curry with handfuls of cilantro and the rice.

2 tablespoons safflower oil
2 onions, peeled and finely chopped
2 cloves garlic, peeled and finely chopped
1 green chile, seeded and finely chopped
2 pounds/1 kg pumpkin, peeled, seeded, and coarsely chopped
1 can (14 ounces/400 g) chickpeas, drained and rinsed
About 1½ cups/250 ml vegetable stock
1½ cups/400 ml coconut milk
Salt
2 handfuls of snow peas
A handful of fresh cilantro

Penne with almond, goat cheese, and parsley pesto

For the pesto
2 cloves garlic, peeled
Salt and pepper
2 large handfuls of fresh
   parsley
½ cup/50 g blanched
   almonds
1 cup/200 g soft goat
   cheese
3 tablespoons olive oil
A squeeze of lemon juice
   or some lemon zest

1½ pounds/750 g fresh or
   dried penne

The bottom line is, it's not really pesto in anything but name. You could also spread this on fish before grilling or pan-frying, or use it to stuff chicken breasts.

In a large mortar and pestle, grind the garlic down with a pinch of salt. Add the parsley and again, grind down until you have a coarse green mixture. Add the almonds and keep grinding, and when you have a coarse paste-like consistency, transfer to a larger bowl. Add the goat cheese and olive oil, combining well. Season, giving the mixture a squeeze of lemon juice or a grating of lemon zest if you feel like it.

Cook the pasta according to the directions on the package. Reserve a tiny bit of the cooking water when you drain, and return the pasta to the pot. Add the pesto and stir to combine, drizzling on some of the cooking water if needed to make sure the pasta is evenly coated.

Fish fingers with tartar sauce and mushy peas

When the volcanic ash from Iceland was drifting across Europe, I was travelling with my husband who was working in Australia. Tragically, we got stranded in Sydney for two whole weeks. We took the ferry every day to Manly Beach, swam, read, and ate. A lot. This reminds me of one of those Manly Beach afternoons, and having to pretend to everyone back in England that we really minded being stuck.

First, make the tartar sauce. In a small mixing bowl, mix the mayonnaise, cornichons, capers, and parsley and squeeze in a dash of lemon juice. Add the horseradish and taste, adjusting accordingly. Season.

Make the mushy peas by cooking the frozen peas in a small pot of water until al dente, a few minutes. Drain, add the peas back to the pan, and squash them with a potato masher. Add the crème fraîche, olive oil, mint, and salt and pepper. Cover and keep to the side.

Cut the fish into finger-sized chunks. Brush a griddle or frying pan with some oil and, when the pan is searing hot, add the fish. Cook for a minute or two on each side. Serve with the mushy peas, tartar sauce, and lemon wedges.

SERVES 2

For the tartar sauce
4 tablespoons mayonnaise
4 small cornichons, finely chopped
1 heaping tablespoon capers
A handful of fresh parsley, finely chopped
A squeeze of lemon juice (keep the rest for wedges)
1 tablespoon grated fresh horseradish
Salt and pepper

For the peas
1 cup/150 g frozen peas
1 tablespoon crème fraîche
1 teaspoon olive oil
A small handful of chopped fresh mint
Salt and pepper

10 ounces/300 g firm-fleshed sustainable white fish, such as pollack (ask your fishmonger)
2 tablespoons olive oil

Overnight lamb

Serve it to someone who appreciates a long night.

Heat a bit of oil in a frying pan over medium to high heat. Brown the lamb in batches if need be or, if you can, all in one go. This should take 5 minutes or so. When thoroughly brown, set aside on a plate.

Over low heat, sweat the onion and garlic for a few minutes, add the anchovies, stir for a few seconds, and then add the stock, followed by the wine. Add the lamb and the rosemary, stir, cover the pan, and cook over low heat for around 30 minutes. Take off the heat and leave the lamb to cool. Cover and store overnight in the fridge.

When you are ready for your lamb supper, take the pan out of the fridge, uncover, and put it back on the stove top (you may need to add a little more stock if it has soaked up the juices in the night). Heat on low, adding the mustard, butter, and half-and-half and stirring it all through until piping hot.

SERVES 4 TO 6

Olive oil

2 pounds/900 g lean lamb, cut into small biteable pieces

1 onion, peeled and finely chopped

2 cloves garlic, peeled and finely chopped

A few anchovy fillets, finely chopped

1 cup/250 ml lamb or chicken stock

¾ cup/185 ml white wine

A handful of chopped fresh rosemary

1 tablespoon Dijon mustard

1 tablespoon butter

1 tablespoon half-and-half

Mushrooms

Vegetable and chicken itame (or an honest stir-fry to the uninitiated!)

In New York I lived near a macrobiotic restaurant that featured a version of this on their menu. It's one of those things to be had when you've been indulging a bit much that will put you back on the straight and narrow.

Heat the sesame oil in a wok until very hot. Add the chicken strips and cook for a few minutes, then repeat the process with the onion, chile, cabbage, bell pepper, mushrooms, carrot, and bean sprouts, flash cooking each thing before adding another. Splash with the tamari and stir. Mix in the coconut cream and add the lime juice. Serve on rice or some soba noodles.

SERVES 2

1 tablespoon sesame oil

5 ounces/150 g skinless and boneless chicken breast, sliced into thin strips

½ onion, peeled and finely chopped

1 red chile, seeded and finely chopped

1 cup/70 g finely shredded green cabbage

1 green bell pepper, finely chopped

¾ cup/70 g chopped mushrooms

1 large carrot, peeled and coarsely grated

A handful of bean sprouts

2 tablespoons tamari (wheat-free soy sauce)

1 tablespoon coconut cream

Juice of 1 lime

Halibut with sorrel sauce and Jerusalem artichoke purée

SERVES 2

For the Jerusalem artichoke purée
9 ounces/250 g Jerusalem
    artichokes
1¼ cups/300 ml milk
1 tablespoon butter
Salt and pepper

2 firm-fleshed sustainable
    white fish fillets, such as
    halibut (ask your
    fishmonger)
Salt and pepper
Olive oil

For the sauce
1 small bunch sorrel
A handful of fresh
    tarragon
2 heaping tablespoons
    crème fraîche
1 tablespoon olive oil
Juice of ½ lemon
Salt and pepper

Halibut is a fish to treat with care and have rarely as, like cod, it is being overfished. It is meaty and wonderful, particularly good served with something soft, à la the artichoke purée or mashed potatoes.

Preheat the oven to 400°F/200°C. Peel the Jerusalem artichokes, place in a saucepan, and pour the milk over them. Cook them over low heat until tender, 10 to 15 minutes. Drain, saving a little bit of the milk, and purée them in the blender with the butter and the reserved milk. Season and keep warm to one side.

Wash and dry the fish and season, brushing with a little olive oil. Heat a griddle or frying pan and, when searing hot, place the fish in it, skin side down. Cook for a few minutes, and then turn and place in the hot oven for 10 minutes.

While the fish is cooking, blanch the sorrel in a saucepan of boiling water for no more than 30 seconds. Quickly submerge into iced water, then drain and squeeze out all the water. Finely chop the sorrel along with the tarragon and, in a small bowl, mix it with the crème fraîche, olive oil, lemon juice, and salt and pepper.

Put the Jerusalem artichoke purée on serving plates, place the fish on top, and serve with a generous dollop of sauce.

The second Mor Mor's chicken

My Mor Mor was not Norwegian at all. She was born Patsy Louise in Packard, Kentucky, in what she called a "hillbilly" coal mining camp. When she married my grandfather, she decided that she liked the name Mor Mor, and that when she was a grandmother, she would take it as her own. And she did.

She had a laugh that traversed years of cigarettes and jokes, and rang out like a deep, dirty well.

Her chicken is the stuff of fable among my aunts, and when I'd talk to them about recipes, they would always bang on about Mor Mor's chicken from their childhood. The problem was, neither of them could really remember what was in it, they just remembered the ultimate result being delicious. They muttered about mushrooms, they muttered about tarragon.

"Ring Mor Mor!" they urged me.

"Mor Mor, what was in your chicken?" I asked Mor Mor, who was sipping her nightly martini in New York.

"Christ, I don't know baby. Chicken?" Mor Mor said.

Mor Mor, coaxed and prodded, didn't remember. She thought it may have something to do with Campbell's Soup, but I'm not so sure, because it sounded disgusting. I resolved that maybe they just all had different taste in the seventies.

She had many incarnations and her name and its changes embodied them. She became Patricia when

Broadway beckoned in the mid 1940s. She would always honor her roots, and she could conjure a country twang in a heartbeat with the throaty voice that would be her lifelong moniker. Her down-home ways and grit were two of the many things that endeared her to Gary Cooper, with whom she co-starred in *The Fountainhead* in 1949. They embarked on a love affair that would devastate both of them. She met my grandfather on the rebound from Cooper in 1951, at a dinner party thrown by Lillian Hellman. He totally ignored her, although he sat next to her, but to her surprise he called her the next morning to ask her out for dinner. She told him she was busy, but he persisted, and after a while she said, recalling it for me years later, she simply ran out of excuses.

They married in New York in 1953, and were to have five children together. Their son Theo was in his baby carriage in New York in 1960 when he was hit by a taxi running a red light. He suffered brain damage that eventually took the family home to their farmhouse in England. Two years later, their seven-year-old daughter Olivia contracted measles encephalitis and died. It is astonishing to look back on Patricia's numerous awards at this time (including an Oscar for best actress in *Hud* in 1963) with the knowledge that her domestic life was dissolving around her. In 1965, pregnant with her fifth child, Lucy, Patricia suffered three cerebral aneurysms, which left her in a coma for nearly a month. When she came round she was left without language or memory, paralyzed on her right side. Her rehabilitation is the stuff of legend, and the courage that she displayed throughout the long, dark days of

(continued)

recovery, undeniable. She learned to walk and talk, read and write all over again, with the support of her husband and neighbors, a martini and cigarette never far from reach. She was nominated for another Academy Award in 1968, for her work in *The Subject Was Roses*. Her homecoming speech, as it were, brought her peers to their feet in a standing ovation, as those whisky chords tumbled over each other to proclaim, "I am so happy to be alive. Alive, alive-O."

Her fervency was real. Her life was one rich with beauty and unbearable injustice. Throughout it all, she retained a stellar sense of humor, faith, and a heart big enough to carry our entire family. She delighted in the simple—the depth of a sunflower, a doggy bag, a loud curse word, or a filthy story. In the dearth of her short-term memory, one was "Darling," "Divine One," or "Beauty," and anyone who has been so addressed by her would know the honor that it carried. She was regal in every inch of her being, even in the face of the cancer that ravaged her. She told my aunt Ophelia that she was "a little offended" she had cancer, and why shouldn't she be? She had been so close to death in her life, danced neatly away from him, and here he was again, darkening her door.

Our beloved Mor Mor died in August 2010 in her own bed, surrounded by her family. She told me she'd be gone before my baby was born, and she was right. The night before, she had dinner with her kids, kissed them each, raised a glass, and told them she'd had "a lovely time."

The secret of her mysterious chicken died with her. The following is my imagined Mor Mor's chicken, in tribute to all of her gutsy glory, beauty, and tenacity. If it was to be eaten and enjoyed Mor Mor style, it would involve copious amounts of corn bread, white wine, and some matinée-idol handsome men to eat it with.

Eat it with the people you love the most, and don't waste it on the dull.

In a large casserole, heat the oil and add the chicken pieces to brown. Turn the pieces after a few minutes to make sure they are evenly colored. When all are brown, add the onion, garlic, bay leaves, herbes de Provence, and chicken stock and cook on a low to medium heat for 10 to 15 minutes. To test doneness, take a piece of chicken out and pierce, making sure the juices run clear. If they don't, put it back and cook for another 5 minutes. When the chicken has cooked, carefully take it out of the casserole and keep to one side.

Leaving the stocky juices, take the onion and garlic out of the casserole and throw them in the compost. Reduce the stock by half by boiling it up and bringing it back down again. Add the wine and season. Add the mushrooms and cook for 5 minutes, and then add the peas and cook for another 3 or 4 minutes. Lastly, gently stir in the cream, and then the herbs. Put the chicken back in the casserole, season, and take to the table. Delicious with mashed potatoes.

SERVES 4

1 tablespoon olive oil

4 skinless, boneless chicken breasts, chopped into bite-size pieces

1 onion, peeled but whole

1 head of garlic, cut in half

2 bay leaves

A pinch of herbes de Provence

5 cups/1.2 liters chicken stock (preferably fresh free-range chicken stock)

½ cup/125 ml white wine

A large pinch of salt

A pinch of pepper

3 cups/250 g wild mushrooms

1½ cups/250 g frozen peas

1¼ cups/300 ml heavy cream

A handful each of fresh parsley, chervil, and tarragon, finely chopped

Spring

I couldn't sleep, and I started to think about the rhubarb poking its sleepy head out in the garden.

In her famous book of household management, the Victorian domestic advisor Isabella Beeton suggests rhubarb only in the form of an economical jam for making in the months of February to April. I am suggesting it as a rice pudding, or on its own, boiled up with a bit of sugar, because it seems such a travesty in the spring not to celebrate rhubarb then and there. If you have an abundance, of course, jam is the sensible way of prolonging the feast.

I am a huge devotee of Mrs. Beeton, the somewhat faceless author of a cookbook that has sold in the millions, and continues to be reprinted and revised, year after year. She styled herself as the original domestic goddess, but her true talent was in entrepreneurship and marketing. Her recipes do little for me, and are pretty unappealing to a modern palate, but I love her unconventional story and spirit. Today, she'd be a multimillionaire. She saw a gap in the market, in the form of the newly growing middle classes, who were looking for a calm, authoritative voice on everything from roasting meat to finding a wet nurse if you were having trouble breastfeeding. The tone she projects in her book is one of matronly competence, but in reality, she was a twenty-three-year-old fashion journalist and editor, a newlywed, more comfortable at an office desk than the oven. She was, however, a keen and adept baker. Brought up in Cheapside, then Epsom, she taps into the subconscious of her urban Victorian reader, suspicious of food adulteration and intensive farming, a reader who yearns at moments for the simple rural idyll that precedes them, their steam trains, servants, and mills.

In her syllabub recipe, Mrs. Beeton invites you to "milk directly into the bowl," as though available cows udders are two a penny in the borough of Bow. What she is getting at remains timeless; the thirst for perfection sought through domestic bibles. We can learn much about history and the habits and dreams of a nation through its old cookbooks. There is Eliza Acton, a marvelous food writer who came before Mrs. Beeton (indeed, Mrs. B shamelessly plagiarized quite a few of her recipes); Ambrose Heath (introduced to me by Peter Begg, a fountain of food knowledge), a waspishly funny columnist for *The Times* and *Guardian* who published books in the 1930s; Alice B. Toklas, wry lover of Gertrude Stein and heavenly food writer and cook;

M.F.K. Fisher, author of novels and studies of food, including the brilliant *Serve It Forth*; Jane Grigson, whose books on vegetables are modern-day classics; Elizabeth David, who brought French Provençal cooking to the masses. These are six food writers who I'm thinking of on the spur of the moment, amidst thoughts of rhubarb and not sleeping. There are myriad others to add to this list, both living and dead. Do explore them if you don't already know them and you love reading about food, because you will be richly rewarded.

We are now in the season of change; embrace it with abandon! The garden is abundant with possibility; spinach and lettuce are in season, tender, and the perfect green foil for the meat you serve them with.

Spring is a time of firsts, warm with romance, bloom, and promise. If you can't be bothered with cooking, make like the French on the first of May and find some lily of the valley, keeping your table as sweet as the changing landscape.

Spring
Breakfasts

Rhubarb rice pudding

SERVES 2

4 cups/1 liter milk, plus
  more as needed
¾ cup/150 g basmati rice
1 cinnamon stick
¼ cup/80 g agave nectar or
  honey
1 teaspoon orange flower
  water

For the rhubarb

12 ounces/350 g rhubarb,
  cut into 1-inch/2.5-cm
  lengths
½ cup/125 ml water
1 star anise
1 teaspoon rose water
2 tablespoons agave
  nectar or honey

I used to pick rhubarb in my granny Gee-Gee's garden when I was about seven, with a bowl of sugar clutched in my fat little hand. The trick was to lick the rhubarb, dip it in the sugar, and crunch away. I would always do it to excess, which was a surefire way to aching guts, and Gee-Gee clucking over me with some milk of magnesia. Prepared this way, you have all the joy without the pain, and if you have access to a bumper crop, follow Mrs. Beeton's example and make some jam. *Pictured on page 119.*

First, make the rice pudding. Pour the milk and rice into a medium-sized saucepan, add the cinnamon stick, bring to a boil, and then simmer over very low heat, stirring frequently, for around 30 minutes. At this point, stir in the agave or honey and orange flower water and cook for another 5 to 10 minutes, adding more milk if the pudding starts looking dry.

In a separate heavy-bottomed saucepan, place the rhubarb, water, star anise, rose water, and agave or honey. Bring to a boil and simmer on low for about 10 minutes, turning once or twice, until you have a lovely tender pink softness. Plate the rice pudding and swirl the rhubarb through.

Zucchini muffins

Celebrating the green of spring, the gold of first sun, and the all-round brilliance that is cheese. You can also serve these for tea with a bit of butter.

Preheat the oven to 375°F/190°C and grease eight cups of two large-capacity muffin pans.

I make this in the stand mixer, but you can do it in a mixing bowl as easily. Start with the dry ingredients, sifting in the flour and baking powder. Slowly add the egg, oil, and milk, whisking all the while. Add the zucchini, cheese, and thyme and season to taste. Pour into the prepared cups and bake for around 20 minutes, or until golden.

MAKES 8 MUFFINS

2 cups/230 g spelt flour
1 teaspoon baking powder
1 egg
¼ cup/60 ml olive oil
⅔ cup/170 ml milk
1 medium-sized zucchini, coarsely grated
1 cup/100 g grated Parmesan cheese
1 tablespoon chopped fresh thyme
Salt and pepper

Halloumi croque madame with black olives

After a very late concert in Paris, from which we spilled out into torrential rain, my husband and I found ourselves in one of those cafés you dream about. Safe from the downpour, we were greeted with deep glasses of red wine and the classic sandwich—oozing slabs of Gruyère atop Poilâne bread, his with ham, mine with an egg. When we were back home, I tried to do the same with some halloumi, which was what I happened to have in the fridge. It wouldn't thrill the French, but it was pretty bloody marvelous all the same. Poilâne bread is so named after the French baker, Lionel Poilâne, and it is made from sourdough starter and stone-ground flours, is naturally fermented, and then baked in a traditional wood-fired oven. A rustic sourdough will do in place of it.

Preheat the broiler to high. Lightly toast the bread under the broiler, butter the slices, and cover each one evenly with one layer of ham and then the halloumi. Chop the olives and press them into the halloumi, as much as you can. Put the slices under the piping hot broiler for 4 minutes or so, or until the cheese is golden and bubbling.

SERVES 2

2 slices of sourdough
   bread or, my favorite,
   Poilâne
1 tablespoon butter
2 slices Serrano ham
Enough halloumi to
   generously cover (about
   3½ ounces/100 g)
6 pitted black olives

Apple and raspberry cereal

SERVES 2

2 cups/200 g old-fashioned oats

1 cup/250 ml water

2 apples (Russets work well here)

A handful of raspberries

Some milk or apple juice, to moisten

A small spoonful of runny honey

This is a bit of a cheat because raspberries really start rearing their heads in early summer, May or June. The crows in my garden would attest to this fact as they are a sucker for berries. However, you can substitute another fruit here, maybe some rhubarb? I love a good Bircher muesli-ish cereal; they are simple as anything, and very virtuous.

The night before, put the oats in a bowl and pour the water on top. Grate the apple onto the oats and add the raspberries. Refrigerate overnight and in the morning moisten with some milk or apple juice. Swirl in the honey and eat.

Spicy eggplant and tomato with poached eggs

This was another dinner thing, served at a party on a warm spring night with some couscous. Like so often with soups and stews that have spent a night in the fridge, they are even better reimagined the following morning. Maybe it was just the hangover, but I looked at this and thought, "Hmm, I bet that would be good with some eggs on top." It was, and remains to be, even stone-cold sober.

Cut the eggplant into bite-size chunks and soak for about 20 minutes in a bowl of cold water with a few large pinches of salt. Drain, rinse, and pat dry.

In a heavy-bottomed frying pan, heat a tablespoon of oil, add the garlic and onion, and cook for a few minutes until softened. Add the eggplant along with the rest of the oil, making sure the eggplant is thoroughly coated, then add the paprika and cook on a very low heat, covered, for about half an hour, turning occasionally. Add the tomatoes, tahini, and brown sugar and cook for another 10 minutes, mixing it all through. Taste and season accordingly. Keep warm to the side.

Poach the eggs in a pan of gently boiling water (a splash of white wine vinegar should stop them separating). You should poach the eggs for about 3 minutes if you want them soft in the middle (5 if you want them stern and unyielding).

At the last moment, add the lemon juice and parsley to the eggplant mixture. Plate in shallow bowls and place the poached eggs on top, with perhaps a hunk of sourdough to sop up the juices.

SERVES 2

1 large eggplant
Salt and pepper
2 tablespoons olive oil
1 clove garlic, peeled and finely chopped
1 onion, peeled and finely chopped
½ teaspoon smoked paprika
1 cup/250 g chopped tomatoes
1 teaspoon tahini
1 teaspoon brown sugar
A splash of white wine vinegar
4 eggs
1 tablespoon lemon juice
A handful of chopped fresh parsley

Avocado nut milk smoothie

SERVES 1

½ ripe avocado

A small handful of
blanched almonds

A few chunks of frozen
peeled banana

1 cup/250 ml cold water or
soy milk

A small spoonful of agave
nectar or honey

When I went on a strange raw food diet, this sort of smoothie was a prominent feature. So was my bum after months of eating avocado and nuts in spades! In a *balanced* way, this is super good for you, and deeply moreish. Just don't start having four under the illusion that they are thinning in any way.

Throw all of the ingredients into the blender and purée until smooth.

Rye cracker breads with horseradish and smoked trout pâté

The credit here goes to the very talented Danish chef and food writer, Trina Hahnemann. I just tinkered with the recipe, and give it to you with huge thanks to her. This is also wonderful as a canapé or starter.

For the pâté, put all of the ingredients in the blender and whiz until smooth. Taste and adjust the seasoning accordingly. Refrigerate for a few hours.

For the rye cracker breads, dissolve the yeast in the warm water in a mixing bowl (or in the bowl of a stand mixer), then add the salt, aniseed, honey, and oil and mix well. Add the rye flour, oats, and half of the wheat flour and mix for 5 minutes (use the dough hook if mixing in the stand mixer). Sprinkle the rest of the wheat flour over the dough and leave it to rise for 15 minutes.

Preheat the oven to 400°F/200°C and line a baking sheet with parchment paper. Knead the dough on a floured work surface, then divide it into ten equal pieces and roll each one into a very thin disk. Lay the disks on the parchment paper, two at a time, and bake for 5 to 8 minutes until crisp. Serve the pâté smeared on the crackers.

SERVES 4

For the pâté
2 smoked trout fillets
¼ cup/50 g soft cream cheese
A pinch of cayenne pepper
Lemon juice, to taste
A tablespoon or so of grated fresh horseradish
1 tablespoon light olive oil
Salt and pepper

For the rye cracker breads
2 teaspoons instant yeast
2 cups/500 ml warm water
1 teaspoon salt
2 teaspoons aniseed
1 teaspoon honey
Scant ½ cup/100 ml sunflower oil
2 cups/200 g rye flour
2 cups/200 g rolled oats
1⅔ cups/250 g whole wheat flour

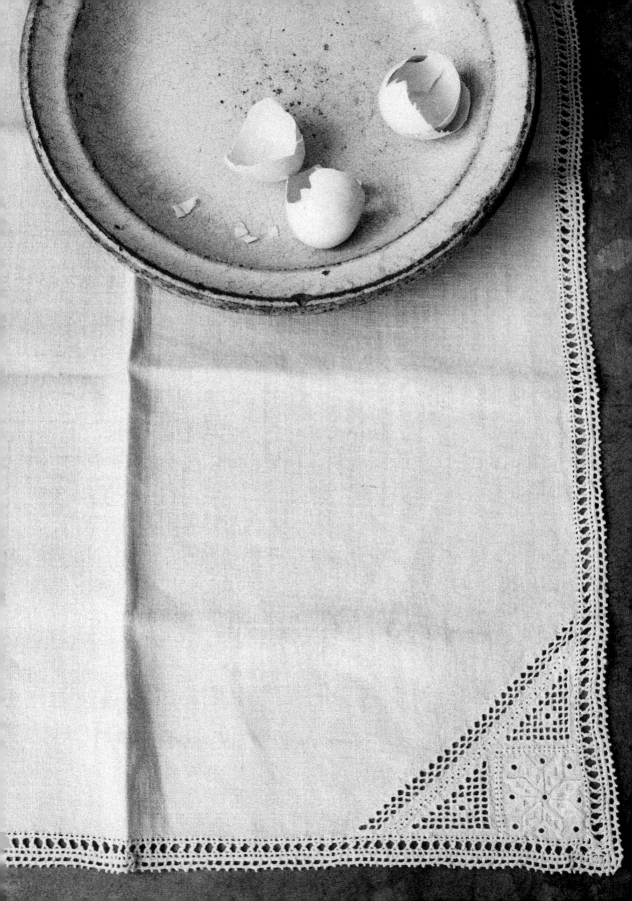

Spring Lunches

Asparagus with hard-boiled eggs, Parmesan, and lemon

There is something totally magical about the lunches of late spring. The first ceremonial throwing open of the windows, or, if you have a garden, venturing a picnic with a layer of thermals.

Asparagus will forever remind me of late spring and early summer in England. I made it last for my girlfriend Emma when she was eight months pregnant and we sat and ate it on her roof. Don't serve it for a romantic lunch—you shouldn't need me to tell you why. And why, oh why, do they ever serve asparagus on airplanes?! I would have this alongside a soup to keep you warm.

SERVES 2

About 12 asparagus spears
2 eggs
2 tablespoons olive oil
¼ cup/25 g grated
   Parmesan cheese
Juice and grated zest of
   ½ lemon
Salt and pepper

Heat a griddle or frying pan over very high heat. Remove the tough ends from the asparagus and cook the spears for about 5 minutes on each side, until browned on the outside and soft within.

While the asparagus is cooking, boil the eggs; about 4 or 5 minutes if you want them still slightly runny inside. Plunge them into cold water, and then peel and chop finely.

Plate the asparagus, pouring over the olive oil and sprinkling with the Parmesan, lemon juice, and zest. Season and sprinkle the hard-boiled eggs on top.

Bruschetta with artichoke purée

SERVES 2

2 medium-sized artichokes

Olive oil

1 clove garlic, peeled and finely chopped

Juice and grated zest of 1 lemon

Salt and pepper

2 thick slices sourdough bread

A small handful of torn fresh basil

These are great things to serve before the main course is ready if you have a lot of people for lunch or dinner, or if you are trying to be grown up and have people over for "drinks." I've never accomplished this. It's either lunch or dinner.

Break off the artichoke stalks and snap or cut off all the leaves. Spoon out the wispy choke and discard. Cut the artichoke hearts into quarters. Heat 3 tablespoons of olive oil in a medium-sized frying pan over medium-low heat and sweat the garlic. Add the artichokes and a teacupful of water and cook on low for about 30 minutes.

When softened, transfer the artichokes to a blender or food processor, add the lemon juice, zest, and a splash more olive oil and purée, then season to taste. Heat a griddle or frying pan until it's searing hot, put in the sourdough, and cook for a minute or two on each side.

Serve the bread spread with the artichoke purée and the torn basil sprinkled on top.

Hot smoked salmon tacos

Some dear friends, now Mr. and Mrs. Collins (not Joan or Phil!), got married last year in a magical place called Cayucos in California. A sleepy seaside town, it held two spectacular gastronomic weapons: salted brown-butter cookies, which would fell a stony-hearted puritan, and tacos, which we ate the day after the wedding at Ruddell's Smokehouse, a tiny wooden shed by the water. The tacos exploded with flavor—enigmatic and intense—and that first bite will live with me until I'm grey and ancient. Here they are for your delectation. The cookies I haven't quite figured out yet, but you can imagine them in the interim.

Mix the mayonnaise and sour cream together in a large mixing bowl and add the chile, cumin, lemon juice, and cilantro. Flake in the hot-smoked salmon and season to taste. Put the mixture into the warmed taco shells and top with shredded cabbage and tomatoes. Serve with lime wedges.

**SERVES 6
HUNGRY PEOPLE**

½ cup/125 g mayonnaise

½ cup/125 g sour cream

1 tablespoon chile powder

1 tablespoon ground
    cumin

2 tablespoons lemon juice

A big handful of chopped
    fresh cilantro

1 pound/450 g hot-smoked
    salmon or any
    smoked fish

Salt and pepper

6 taco shells, warmed

A handful of shredded red
    cabbage

2 tomatoes, finely chopped

2 limes, cut into wedges

Butter lettuce, lobster, and crayfish salad

SERVES 4

For the dressing
1 tablespoon white wine
    vinegar
½ teaspoon Dijon mustard
½ teaspoon agave nectar or
    superfine sugar
5 tablespoons light
    olive oil
3 tablespoons sour cream
Juice of 1 lemon
A handful of chopped fresh
    tarragon and/or chervil
Salt and pepper

1 head butter lettuce
1½ cups/235 g fresh or
    frozen peas
1 pound/450 g cooked
    lobster meat
9 ounces/250 g cooked
    crayfish meat or
    shelled shrimp
1 large avocado (with no
    brown bits please)
A handful of pea shoots

Everything about this just works. Sweet, creamy, and hearty, it would work as a stand-alone lunch on a warm day. You could also make it as a starter for a dinner party. It makes me think of Oslo, a place that I love and that I visited for the first time only two years ago, which is odd because half of my family hails from there. I could live in the lovely clean airport, where you can get open-faced rye sandwiches galore, piled high with crayfish and mayonnaise. Yum. You can also use the dressing on a cold piece of grilled chicken.

To make the dressing, put the vinegar, mustard, and agave or sugar in a mixing bowl and stir in the olive oil. When emulsified, add the sour cream, lemon, and herbs. Season to taste.

Tear the lettuce leaves from the head and carefully wash and dry them. Put the lettuce into a big, low bowl so you can admire the beauty of the salad. Cook the peas very briefly in boiling salted water, literally a minute or two, so they're tender. Drain them and leave to cool.

Chop the lobster meat and add it and the crayfish to the bowl. Pour on the peas. Just before you serve, peel, pit, and slice the avocado into half moons and add to the bowl. Dress the salad and add the pea shoots.

Crespéou

For the yellow omelet
5 eggs
1 tablespoon half-and-half
Salt and pepper
Olive oil
1 small onion, peeled and
    finely chopped
A pinch of saffron

For the green omelet
5 eggs
Salt and pepper
Olive oil
A handful of baby spinach
3 tablespoons chopped
    fresh tarragon
1 tablespoon chopped
    fresh parsley
¼ cup/25 g grated
    Parmesan cheese

For the red omelet
5 eggs
Salt and pepper
Olive oil
8 cherry tomatoes,
    quartered
¼ cup/25 g crumbled soft
    goat cheese

Chopped fresh soft herbs,
    to garnish

Crespéou is a Provençal omelet cake in essence, with each layer offering a different color and flavor. It is a useful thing for a big brunch-type occasion where you have many to feed; make it the day before and pop in the fridge overnight. You can be creative with a crespéou and mix and match the fillings—the ones I've picked are the things I happened to have on hand. *Pictured on pages 144–145.*

To make the yellow omelet, whisk the eggs with the half-and-half and season. Heat a splash of olive oil in a small to medium-sized nonstick frying pan, add the onion, and to it the saffron. Stir and cook until the onion is translucent. Pour in the whisked eggs and cook until set. When it is totally set, place the omelet on a plate.

To make the green omelet, whisk the eggs and season. Heat the oil in the pan and add the spinach, tarragon, and parsley. Add the eggs and Parmesan and cook until set. Place on top of the yellow omelet.

To make the red omelet, whisk the eggs and season. Heat a splash of olive oil in the pan. Sauté the tomatoes for a minute or so, moving them around with a spatula, and then add the eggs. Add the goat cheese and cook until set. Place on top of the green omelet.

Wrap the three stacked omelets in waxed paper and then wrap in a layer of aluminum foil, pressing them down. Refrigerate overnight and unwrap just before serving with more chopped herbs thrown on top. Cut as you would a cake and serve with a green salad.

Pea, pesto, and arugula soup

This is quite a useful thing to have in the back of your head if people happen to show up uninvited, although I only ever seem to have eggs in the house when that happens to me, and I have to pretend that, yes, I really did mean to make a frittata for dinner. The soup is dead quick, yet delicious, and hopefully the uninvited will provide their own dessert, or at least have brought some chocolate.

Place all of the pesto ingredients in a blender or food processor and whiz up until you have a green, bubbly sauce, adding a splash of water if the pesto is a little thick. Taste, season, and adjust anything that needs adjusting.

In a large saucepan, heat the olive oil and soften the onion. Add the zucchini, then pour in the stock and simmer on low for 8 to 10 minutes. Add the peas and arugula, bring back to a boil, and cook for another 3 or 4 minutes until the vegetables are tender.

Let the soup cool for 15 minutes or so and then, in careful batches, mix in a blender until you have a velvety purée. Reheat in the saucepan or serve cold, as it works either way. You can either run 4 tablespoons of pesto through the soup when you're serving or reheating, if you are. Or, if serving cold, add it to the blender when you are puréeing the batches.

SERVES 4

For the pesto
A large handful of fresh
    basil leaves
1 clove garlic, peeled and
    roughly chopped
A few tablespoons of pine
    nuts
4 tablespoons olive oil
¼ cup/25 g grated
    Parmesan cheese
Salt and pepper

1 tablespoon olive oil
1 small onion, peeled and
    finely chopped
2 small zucchini, chopped
3½ cups/875 ml chicken or
    vegetable stock
1 package (1 pound/450 g)
    frozen peas
A large handful of arugula

Potato pancakes with smoked salmon and a cucumber and dill salad

MAKES 8 PANCAKES

For the cucumber salad
½ cucumber, peeled and
   thinly sliced into rounds
1 tablespoon buttermilk
1 tablespoon light olive oil
1 teaspoon white wine
   vinegar
A squeeze of lemon juice
Salt and pepper
A small handful of
   chopped fresh dill

These remind me of being a child. I grew up with a Scottish nanny named Maureen who is not only the best person in the world, but also one of the cleverest—she boasted a Mensa membership. My brothers and sister and I used to go to Maureen's mum and dad's house in Edinburgh every Hogmanay, until we were too teenage and complaining, and her dad, Pop, used to make us potato pancakes with fried eggs and mushrooms for breakfast. He also played the bones, and would clack out a tune on the sideboard as the eggs sizzled. We used to steal liqueur chocolates from the sideboard and pretend we were drunk.

Every piece of random general knowledge I possess is from Maureen, and she taught me to tie my shoelaces. *Pictured on page 149.*

Make the cucumber salad by assembling the cucumber rounds onto a big plate and mixing the buttermilk, olive oil, white wine vinegar, lemon, and salt and pepper together into a dressing in a small bowl. Pour the dressing over the cucumber and garnish with dill, reserving a bit for the salmon.

To make the potato pancakes, in a mixing bowl, mix together the mashed potato, flour, baking soda, and a pinch of salt, then beat in the buttermilk. Grate the potato, squeezing out any liquid; add into the mix with the parsley and season with salt and pepper.

Heat a griddle or frying pan and melt the butter. Ladle in the potato pancake batter, in batches if need be, making individual hotcake-sized rounds. Fry them for 3 to 5 minutes until burnished and brown, then turn and cook for a couple of minutes longer. Lay the pancakes on a plate, make a curl of salmon on top of each one, dot with crème fraîche and dill, and serve the cucumber salad on the side. Drizzle the remaining dressing over the salmon, if you like.

For the potato pancakes
⅔ cup/125 g mashed
    potato
Scant ½ cup/50 g spelt
    flour
¼ teaspoon baking soda
Salt and pepper
Scant ½ cup/100 ml
    buttermilk
1 potato (about 3½ ounces/
    100 g), peeled
A small handful of
    chopped fresh parsley
1 tablespoon butter

7 ounces/200 g smoked
    salmon
3 tablespoons crème
    fraîche

Spring
Suppers

Macky Boy's mackerel with horseradish dressing

SERVES 2

2 smoked mackerel fillets
1 tablespoon runny honey
A glug of olive oil
2 teaspoons capers

For the salad

1 tablespoon olive oil
1 teaspoon white wine
    vinegar
1 heaping teaspoon
    finely grated fresh
    horseradish
A squeeze of lemon juice
2 heaping tablespoons
    crème fraîche
Salt and pepper
2 handfuls of baby spinach

My friend and neighbor Mac is a photographer by trade, but he also cooks a mean dinner, and the ladies love him for it. If I'm feeling particularly deluded, I start feeling a bit Wendy to the Lost Boys and will cook for the entire street. Sometimes this extends to cooking Mac a fry-up, as he gets a very hungry, haunted look in the morning. He cooked me mackerel brushed with honey to return the favor, and it turned into this. He tells me that my crumble is "Article lick!" and like a lot of West Indian and island sayings, it sings what it means. This saying has been shortened in my house to "It's the lick," when something's brilliant.

Preheat the oven to 400°F/200°C. Place the mackerel on some aluminum foil on a baking sheet. Brush the mackerel on both sides with the honey and place in the hot oven. Cook for 10 minutes or so.

In the meantime, heat the olive oil in a small frying pan and when it's searing hot, add the capers. Fry the capers until they are crispy, and leave them in the pan.

For the salad, make the dressing by mixing together the oil and vinegar and slowly whisking in the horseradish, lemon, and crème fraîche. Season to taste, then dress the spinach. Or, serve the horseradish on the side as a cream by slowly whisking the horseradish and lemon into the crème fraîche instead of into the oil and vinegar and season to taste. Serve the mackerel on top of the spinach, dotted with capers and accompanied by the horseradish cream.

Coconut and crab rice with lime and cilantro

SERVES 2

1 tablespoon sunflower oil

1 teaspoon coriander seeds

1 teaspoon cumin seeds or ground cumin

1 small onion, peeled and finely chopped

1 small red chile, seeded and finely chopped

1 green onion, finely chopped

1 cup/250 ml coconut milk

1 cup/250 ml fish stock

1½ cups/275 g basmati rice

Salt and pepper

¾ cup/170 g cooked crabmeat

A small handful of fresh cilantro, chopped

Juice and grated zest of 1 lime

This is another one of those easy spring dishes. You could also run a tablespoon of yogurt through for some cool among the chile.

In a medium-sized saucepan (with a tight-fitting lid), heat the oil. Add to it the coriander seeds and cumin, then the onion, chile, and green onion. Stir for a few minutes, coating the onions with the spicy oil. Pour in the coconut milk and fish stock and add the rice. Season, bring to a rolling boil, and, as soon as this happens, put the lid on and bring the heat right down. Cook for 10 minutes. Take off the heat, fluff the rice, and add the crab meat, chopped cilantro, and the lime juice and zest. Serve.

Pollack with Indian spices and yogurt-lime dressing

A fragrant way to tart up a piece of fish. Serve with basmati rice tempered with a cardamom pod or two, and some buttered steamed spinach. If you finish with rose petal ice cream, you're in for a happy night. *Pictured on pages 160–161.*

Put the coriander, cumin, and fenugreek in a small frying pan and dry-roast over medium heat for a couple of minutes until they smell aromatic. Transfer them to a mortar and pestle, add the ginger, cinnamon, salt, and peppercorns, and bash together until you have a rough powder. Rub this mix into the pollack and leave to one side.

Make the dressing by mixing the yogurt, lime juice and zest, and cilantro together in a small mixing bowl. Season to taste.

Heat a griddle or frying pan until searing hot and place the pollack on it. Cook the fish for about 4 minutes on each side. Serve with rice and a salad, with the yogurt dressing draping off the pollack.

SERVES 4

1 teaspoon coriander seeds
1 teaspoon cumin seeds
1 teaspoon fenugreek seeds
½ teaspoon ground ginger
A pinch of ground cinnamon
Sea salt
A few black peppercorns
4 pollack fillets

For the yogurt dressing
4 to 6 tablespoons Greek yogurt, strained
Juice and grated zest of 1 lime
A small handful of finely chopped fresh cilantro
Salt and pepper

Lemony lentil soup

I was inspired to make this after going to a Persian restaurant late at night and eating a lentil soup heavy with lemon. Theirs was hot, and quite thin. I liked the idea of making it almost like a stew, something you could possibly toss some rice and yogurt into, with lots of cilantro. It's a meal in itself. I like that kind of one-stop eating.

In a large, heavy-bottomed pot, cover the lentils with 4 cups/1 liter of the stock and add the bay leaves. Bring to a boil, and then simmer over low heat, uncovered, for 30 to 40 minutes, until the lentils are very soft.

While the lentils are cooking, heat the olive oil in a frying pan. Gently sweat the onion and green onions over low heat for around 10 minutes, and then add the celery. Sprinkle on the cumin and stir, cooking for another 5 minutes or so and adding a little more olive oil if necessary. Add this mix to the lentils along with the lemon juice. Remove the bay leaves and season to taste.

Let everything cool for a bit, then transfer to the blender and purée, adding the extra stock or water to adjust the consistency. Depending on the size of your blender, you may have to do this in two batches.

Pour the soup back into the washed pot and reheat on low, adding the spinach and half of the cilantro. Season to taste again.

Serve at room temperature with some more lemon juice and olive oil, the remaining cilantro and, if you have some, a swirl of Greek yogurt.

SERVES 6

2 cups/500 g red lentils

4 cups/1 liter vegetable or chicken stock, plus 1 cup/250 ml stock or water

3 bay leaves

2 tablespoons olive oil, plus extra for serving

½ onion, peeled and finely chopped

2 green onions, white part only, finely chopped

2 celery stalks, finely chopped

1 tablespoon ground cumin

Juice of 3 lemons, plus extra for serving

Salt and pepper

2 cups/100 g spinach, coarsely chopped

½ cup/20 g finely chopped fresh cilantro

Paella

SERVES 8

Olive oil

4 skinless, boneless
chicken breasts, cut into
bite-size pieces

3½ ounces/100 g chorizo,
sliced

1 onion, peeled and finely
chopped

3 cloves garlic, peeled and
finely chopped

A large pinch of saffron

5 cups/1.2 liters chicken
stock, warmed

2 cups/500 g Spanish
short-grain paella rice

¼ teaspoon dried red chile
flakes

4 large tomatoes, seeded
and chopped

8 or so jumbo shrimp

8 or so scallops

2 cups/310 g frozen peas

A handful of fresh parsley

1 lemon, cut into wedges

Good paella can be a bit of a Holy Grail, and everyone argues about what should go into it. Given that I don't eat chorizo, I should probably not add my voice to the clamor for the risk of being stoned. But here it is anyway, inspired by a trip to Barcelona and an old-fashioned seafood restaurant with green tiles and smoky mirrors.

Heat 1 tablespoon of oil in a big, deep frying pan and sauté the chicken pieces until browned, adding the chorizo to cook for the last few minutes. Add the onion and garlic and sweat for another few minutes. In a mixing bowl, mix the saffron into your warm stock and let it infuse for a couple of minutes. Adding more oil to the pan, stir in the rice and pour in half of the saffron-infused stock. Add the chile flakes and tomatoes and cook on a lowish heat for around 20 minutes, stirring occasionally.

Just toward the end, add the rest of the chicken stock and the shrimp and scallops and cook for another 5 minutes with a lid on the pan. Lastly, add the peas and cook for another 4 minutes or so. Serve with heaped parsley, a dash of olive oil, and lemon wedges.

Chicken Kiev

I was talking with some friends about nostalgic food from childhood. Sherbet dips, Hula Hoops, and that ubiquitous menu staple from the eighties, the Chicken Kiev. We all agreed that the advent of chicken Kiev was about the most exciting thing ever—that first slice into the plump chicken breast, followed by a hot waft of garlic and pool of molten green butter. I wondered whether you could make a healthy one, and was there even a point? Having trialled this, I think so, and friends' kids might even agree.

Preheat the oven to 400°F/200°C.

Make a mixture of the hummus, 2 tablespoons of the olive oil, and parsley, and leave to the side. Don't overmix as you don't want the oil too incorporated into the hummus. With a very sharp knife, make a narrow slice through the side of the chicken breasts. This will create a small pocket in which to stuff the hummus mixture. Push the mixture in with a spoon and then close the pocket with your fingers. Put the stuffed chicken breasts in the fridge and leave for half an hour.

When you take them out, dredge each breast in the spelt flour, brush with the beaten egg, and then coat with the rye bread crumbs. Take a large frying pan, heat the remaining olive oil over medium heat, and fry the breasts for a few minutes until they are evenly golden. Transfer to a baking sheet and bake for 20 minutes.

SERVES 4

4 tablespoons hummus
Olive oil
A small handful of chopped fresh parsley
4 skinless, boneless chicken breasts
3 tablespoons spelt flour
1 egg, beaten
1 cup/100 g rye bread crumbs

The Sheriff's marinated lamb

SERVES 6

1 bone-in leg of lamb
(about 4½ pounds/2 kg)
A small handful of fresh
finely chopped rosemary
1 teaspoon mustard
powder
About 2 tablespoons finely
chopped fresh ginger
1 teaspoon soy sauce
A small handful of fresh
chopped mint
1 teaspoon white wine
vinegar
1 teaspoon demerara sugar
3 cloves garlic, peeled

Everyone kept telling me that my father-in-law, John, had an incredible lamb recipe. I rang him, my culinary detective nose on the hunt.

"May I have your lamb recipe for my book?" I asked.

"Lamb recipe? Do I have one?" he answered, shades of Mor Mor sending my heart to my boots. It turned out, after much haranguing, that he actually did, but it was mostly in his head. While he will not win awards for his recipe writing, which I have adapted here, he may win one for the lamb itself, being an all-round good egg and the High Sheriff of Somerset, and finally, along with his friend Dave, for being the most devoted Swindon Town supporter ever. *Pictured on page 169.*

Put the lamb in a large roasting tray. For a bone-in leg of lamb, leave on the string until after the meat is cooked (you can also make this with a boneless leg of lamb). Prepare the lamb by making little punctures in the skin with a small knife.

Place the rosemary in a large mortar and pestle with all the other ingredients except the garlic. Give the marinade a good grind, and then, with your fingers, massage it into the lamb. Slice the garlic into small rounds and push them into the pockets that you have cut into the lamb. Cover the lamb and leave it somewhere cool for 2 hours, or longer.

About half an hour before cooking, preheat the oven to 450°F/230°C. Put the lamb in and roast for 20 minutes to brown, then turn down the oven to 400°F/200°C. Cook for about another 1 hour and 20 minutes for lamb that is juicy and pink in the middle. (Add 15 minutes if you like it well-done.) Let the lamb rest for about 15 minutes before carving.

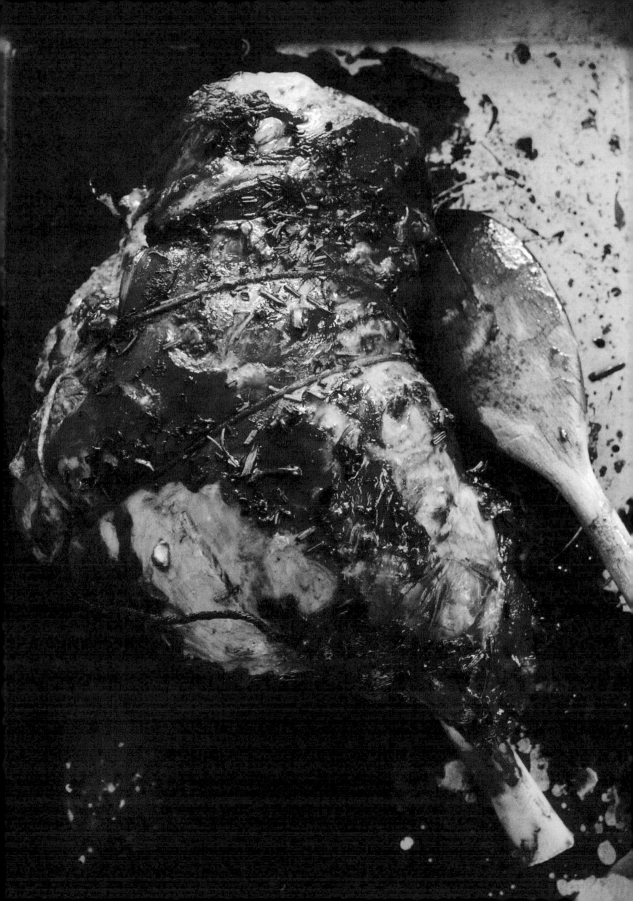

Summer

There is something lulling and rhythmic about August. The summer has sloped into its routine and everyone has, by then, either found their feet or lost their shoes. It is a time for brief, heady love. If you're a teenager, perhaps with a person whose language escapes you, but whose eyes say it all. If you are older, but maybe not wiser, it's a place, a meal, a time, which swoops you up and makes you giddy, cradling you in the transient cup of infatuation. It was famously written about, this summer malady, in books from *Tender is the Night* to *Bonjour Tristesse*, and captured in a jam jar with Joss, the heroine of *The Greengage Summer*. Everything seems possible in the summer: love, escape, and even loss. Grief feels wrong in the heat.

In hot lapses, I've fallen in love with houses that I will never see again, stolen a wooden sailboat (and returned it), and briefly written my life into a town that is now a murmur of Italian that I can't quite hear. All in the name of summer. It is cathartic, this once-a-year release when you can shed your skin under an olive grove, or on a pier with a big wheel blaring color and pop songs.

The food of summer is equally memorable: ambling lunches eaten outside, a table with grilled meats and vegetables with smoky sauces, followed by plates of plump strawberries and peaches and light-as-air lemon mousse. Or the sharp sting of vinegar on fish and chips, demolished on a stone wall by a shingle beach, cold beer the perfect mate to it. Vanilla ice cream was made to be guzzled after swimming in the sea, the salt on your fingers tempering the sugar. It's hard to pick a favorite summer food memory, but up there would be the lobster and crabs legs we ate on my brother's birthday, on a tiny wooden deck in a fishing port in Massachusetts. We ate from paper plates, with tubs of melted butter and a great mess of coleslaw and summer corn on the side. His girlfriend had made some gooey fudge brownies, and they finished the feast. All my summer food memories seem to contain a brownie at the end. Last summer was no exception.

I had the total luxury of being on a small fishing boat off the coast of Dorset in England with the wonderful cook Hugh Fearnley-Whittingstall and his fishing partner, Nick Fisher. It was my husband and I and a small group of friends. It was a rare cloudless day, the sort that Laurie Lee would write of. We fished for mackerel, which are abundant in those waters, and ate them as sashimi, thinly sliced with a smear of wasabi. Some hours later, we came across some scallop divers who sold us a few of their trove. Those we cooked on an open grill on the half shell, with some wild garlic, lemon zest, and chile, a hunk of sourdough bread, baked fresh that morning, to sop up the juice.

I don't remember who suggested the swim; I think it began as a dare as the waters that far out, even in July, are pretty arctic. If we were to undertake it, the prize was a brownie, molten and dense, with a steaming cup of tea. Hugh dove in like an otter, dipping under the boat for an anxious minute. I was in my knickers and an old T-shirt and I teetered on the edge of the boat. I took a deep breath and surrendered, disappearing into water so cold that I swore like a sailor when I finally came up to meet the surface. The brownie that heralded the shuddering return to the boat was manna, the strong tea its perfect partner.

On the drive home, we splayed out in the car, freckled, salt-stained, and replete. Nick Drake sang "Pink Moon" on the radio. It was how life should be.

Summer Breakfasts

Fruit salad with orange flower syrup and mint

SERVES 2 TO 4

For the syrup
2 tablespoons water
1 tablespoon agave nectar
    or honey
1 teaspoon orange flower
    water

1 kiwi, peeled and cut into
    half moons
½ small pineapple, skin
    removed, fruit chopped
    into bite-size pieces
1 ripe mango, peeled
    and chopped
Seeds of 1 pomegranate
½ papaya, peeled, seeded
    and chopped
A handful of fresh mint

Does what it says on the box. The syrup is also really good poured on a lemon cake that's a day or two old. *Pictured on page 177.*

First, make the syrup by placing a small pan over low to medium heat. Add the water, agave or honey, and orange flower water and simmer, reducing for a few minutes until you have a syrup. Leave to the side and let cool.

Put the fruit in a bowl deserving of it. Chop the mint and add it to the mix, lastly pouring the cooled syrup on top. Voilà!

Grilled peaches with ricotta and toasted pistachios

I love grilling or roasting fruit. It brings out a latent cushiony sweetness that is perfectly met with cheese or crème fraîche. Grilled or roasted fruit also works wonders when you're looking for a light, summery dessert.

Preheat a grill or griddle pan until very hot or heat the broiler. Rub the peaches with the butter. Place them on the grill or griddle pan or under the broiler on a heavy heatproof pan and sear for a few minutes on either side, until soft and juicy on the inside and golden on the outside. Plate and drizzle with the runny honey and the ricotta. In a pan, toast the pistachios for a minute or so and sprinkle over the peaches.

SERVES 2

2 peaches, pitted and halved

1 tablespoon butter

1 tablespoon runny dark honey

2 tablespoons ricotta cheese

A handful of shelled unsalted pistachios

Tomato, tofu, and basil scramble

Some people are appalled by tofu. I don't know this, but I imagine Adrian Gill is, in a laconic, laid-back sort of way. Clarissa Dickson Wright would point-blank ignore it, possibly making it sit in the corner, and Gordon Ramsay would set it on fire, calling it a bastard. I am not appalled by tofu. I like it very much, particularly scrambled on toast.

Heat the oil in a frying pan and add the garlic, stirring for a minute. Add the tomatoes and basil, and cook on low for 2 minutes. Add the tomato purée. Crumble in the tofu and the feta and mix it all through, adding a little vegetable stock if the mixture starts to look dry. Taste and season accordingly.

SERVES 2

1 tablespoon olive oil
1 clove garlic, peeled and
  finely chopped
4 medium-large heirloom
  tomatoes, chopped
A handful of fresh coarsely
  torn basil
1 tablespoon tomato purée
About ½ block/160 g
  firm tofu
¼ cup/30 g crumbled feta
  cheese
A splash of vegetable
  stock
Salt and pepper

Rory's savory pancakes

SERVES 2

For the filling
2 handfuls of spinach
Olive oil
½ cup/110 g soft goat
    cheese
A small handful of finely
    chopped fresh parsley
Salt and pepper

For the pancakes
1 cup/115 g spelt flour
1 egg
½ cup/125 ml milk
2 tablespoons olive oil

I was on a very noisy bus with Rory, who plays the trumpet. We were travelling through Germany, talking about food.

"Can I have a recipe named after me in your book?" he asked.

"Yes. Do you want a savory breakfast crêpe named after you? I've got one of those going spare," I said.

He got very excited. "Yes! Yes! A breakfast cake!"

At that moment our bus was stopped and searched by some very polite German policemen, so the conversation ended there. We assured them we were not drug smugglers, and they took our word for it. The breakfast cake was never mentioned again, until now.

Sorry, this is not a breakfast cake, Roar.

First, make the filling. In a 9-inch frying pan over medium heat, wilt the spinach with a little bit of olive oil. Cool and then put in a blender or food processor with the goat cheese, parsley, and salt and pepper to taste and whiz until blended.

Make the pancake batter by mixing together the flour, egg, milk, and 1 tablespoon of the olive oil until you have a smooth batter. Heat the remaining olive oil in a frying pan and add a ladleful of batter. Turn and tilt the pan so the batter covers it evenly. The pancake should be thick enough to hold the filling but not so fat that it is lumpy. Cook the pancake for 2 or 3 minutes until the underside is lacy golden brown. Flip it over with a spatula. Cook on the second side for a minute or so, until brown and lacy. Remove from the heat and transfer to a plate while you make the other pancakes. When you have used up all your batter, gently spread some filling down the middle of each pancake with a spatula. Then roll the pancakes up and eat swiftly.

Fennel frittata

SERVES 2

4 eggs
1 fennel bulb, with a few of
    the fronds
2 tablespoons olive oil
Salt and pepper
About ¼ cup/20 g grated
    Parmesan cheese

Fennel is a generous, diplomatic vegetable that works pretty much anywhere. Conjure up *The Talented Mr. Ripley*, pre–all the murderous action, and eat this frittata pretending you're on the Amalfi Coast. You can serve it cold and with a tomato salad for lunch or supper, too.

Preheat the broiler to high. Whisk the eggs in a bowl.

Peel off the tough outer layers of the fennel and discard. Thinly slice the bulb so you have thin ribbons, and then further chop it down so it is in bite-size pieces.

Heat an ovenproof frying pan and add the olive oil, and then add the fennel. Stir for a few minutes, until the color turns slightly translucent, and then add the whisked eggs and some salt and pepper. Cook until the bottom sets, sprinkle with the grated Parmesan, and then pop the pan under the broiler until the frittata is risen and triumphant, which should take 3 or 4 minutes at most. Serve quickly, garnished with a few fennel fronds.

Strawberry pancakes

The first cookbook I ever owned was *The Winnie-the-Pooh-Cookbook*, and in it was a lovely recipe for pancakes. They are universally appealing and there remains something childishly pleasing about finding fruit in them. I like substituting blueberries here, too.

In a mixing bowl, mix together the ricotta, milk, and egg yolks. Sift in the flour and baking powder.

In a separate bowl, whisk the egg whites and, just before they are stiff, fold them into the first mixing bowl.

Heat the oil in a frying pan until hot and pour in the batter in 3- to 4-inch/10-cm circles. When they begin to look pinpricked, sprinkle some strawberries into the pancakes and, when set, turn them. They should take about 2 minutes on each side. Serve with more strawberries and maple syrup.

SERVES 2

1 cup/225 g ricotta cheese
½ cup/125 ml milk
2 eggs, separated
1 cup/115 g spelt flour
1 teaspoon baking powder
2 tablespoons vegetable oil
A handful of strawberries, hulled and finely chopped
Maple syrup, to serve

Carrot and cream cheese muffins

I suppose that this is a bit of an excuse to have what is really a cake in pretend, pseudo-healthy breakfast form. Sometimes life calls for breakfast cake—it just does—especially when you are pregnant and your legs hurt and your feet have grown a whole size.

Preheat the oven to 375°F/190°C. Grease a standard muffin pan.

To make the muffins, beat the eggs, sugar, and oil with an electric mixer until incorporated. Into a separate bowl, sift together the flour, baking soda, and spices. Roughly chop the walnuts and add them to the dry ingredients along with the grated carrots. Fold the dry ingredients into the beaten egg mixture and slowly mix in the warm water.

Spoon the batter into the prepared muffin pan and bake for 25 minutes.

For the cream cheese icing, in a bowl, whisk together the cream cheese, confectioners' sugar, and vanilla, then add the lemon juice and zest.

When the muffins are cool, ice with the cream cheese icing and sprinkle with cinnamon, if desired.

MAKES 12 MUFFINS

For the muffins

2 eggs
Scant 1 cup/200 g superfine sugar
¾ cup/185 ml sunflower oil
1¼ cups/160 g self-rising flour
1 teaspoon baking soda
2 teaspoons ground cinnamon, plus extra for dusting (optional)
2 teaspoons pumpkin pie spice
½ cup/50 g walnuts
1½ cups/235 g peeled and grated carrots
⅓ cup/80 ml warm water

For the cream cheese icing

9 ounces/250 g cream cheese, softened
¼ cup/60 g confectioners' sugar
Vanilla extract
Juice and grated zest of 1 lemon

Summer Lunches

BIG FAT FEAST

There are few things better than a great heaving table in the garden of a summer, particularly when it's a table filled with things you actually want to eat. I'm sure British readers will remember with a wry smile the lukewarm picnic offerings of years gone by, an indelibly comic part of some English summers: quease-inducing coronation chicken; the ubiquitous poached salmon, spiked with flecks of cucumber and an army of bones to choke the vicar; eggs of dubious age suspended in melting aspic; warm Pimms; and Eton mess left out to curdle and splay, a bit like the skirt of a gin-breathed teacher riding dangerously high from the egg-and-spoon race.

But a summer table filled with delicious choices and Mediterranean influences—now that's a table I can get with. One of the dishes in this section, the octopus, green bean and potato salad, comes straight from the epicenter of this type of eating, its provenance the kitchen of a magical small hotel in Umbria. Others are transported from happy memory to the page: tzatziki made by a big mama in an enormous swimming costume on a small fishing boat off the coast of Greece; radishes from the farmers' market cut wafer thin and dusted with truffle salt and mint (don't panic, truffle salt is relatively inexpensive, and is a fiscally manageable way to conjure up the real thing); kebabs held in sticky fingers, dripping with a garlicky almond dressing; golden beets hot with cayenne; ceviche, conjuring Mexico (for an island flavor, add a dash of coconut milk); and salted sheep's cheese flamed with the aniseed magic of ouzo. I'm convinced the flaming sheep's cheese we ate in a restaurant in Los Angeles is what sent my sister Clover into labor, and immediately after having her son, my gorgeous nephew Finley, she called to find out where we could get some more, and how quickly.

What to drink with this medley? God, anything from a beer with a wedge of lime to a sparkling Pinot Noir. For the teetotaler, pink lemonade or iced tea made with Earl Grey or jasmine tea would do very well. You don't need a garden or a big table to serve your feast on—a rug on the floor would do just as well, and you'll be safe from wasps and that bit closer to the large nap that you'll need anyway.

For me, each of these things contains the very essence of summer, whether you're home or away.

Sheep's cheese with flaming ouzo

You want to use a hard sheep's cheese here, something like Greek kasseri.

I recommend doing this in a big nonstick frying pan. Heat the pan until searing hot, brush with a few drops of olive oil and put in the cheese. Sizzle! Cook it on both sides until golden brown and crispy at the edges. When the cheese is cooked, pour the ouzo into the pan and light with a fire lighter, standing well, well back as the flames can shoot up. Serve flaming at the table and, when the flames have gone out, squeeze the lemon over the cheese and devour!

SERVES 2

2 tablespoons olive oil

7 ounces/200 g kasseri cheese, cut into palm-sized wedges

2 tablespoons ouzo

1 lemon, halved

Tzatziki

SERVES 4

1 cucumber
Salt and pepper
1 cup/250 g goat's milk
  yogurt or Greek yogurt
2 cloves garlic, peeled and
  finely chopped
1 tablespoon smoked olive
  oil
Juice and zest of ½ lemon
A handful of fresh mint,
  finely chopped

Peel and seed the cucumber, and then coarsely grate it. Place it in a colander over the sink and mix it with a few pinches of salt. Leave to drain for about 20 minutes or so, and then pat dry with a kitchen towel.

Put the cucumber in a mixing bowl and add to it the yogurt and garlic, stirring it all through. Add the olive oil, lemon zest, and a few squeezes of lemon juice. Season to taste and then add the mint. *Pictured on page 197.*

Radishes with truffle salt, mint, and olive oil

Wash the radishes and finely shave them. Put the radishes in a bowl and sprinkle them with the truffle salt. Pour over the olive oil and add the mint. *Pictured on pages 200–201.*

SERVES 2 TO 4

A basket of radishes

A pinch of truffle salt

1 tablespoon light olive oil

A small handful of chopped fresh mint

Ceviche with shrimp and avocado

Place the shrimp in a large glass mixing bowl and squeeze the lime juice over them, mixing it all in to make sure the shrimp are covered in juice. Add the tomatoes, green onions, and fresh and dried chile. Add the herbs. Cover the bowl and refrigerate for at least an hour or so. Pit, peel, and chop the avocados and add just before serving so they don't get brown and raddled.

SERVES 4

1 ¼ lb/600 g peeled
   raw shrimp

Juice of 3 limes

2 ripe tomatoes, finely
   chopped

2 green onions, finely
   chopped

1 red chile, seeded and
   finely chopped

A pinch of dried red chile
   flakes

A small handful of
   chopped fresh parsley

A small handful of
   chopped fresh cilantro

2 ripe avocados

PRAWNS

Grilled octopus with potatoes and fagiolini pesto

Grigliata di polpo con patate e pesto di fagiolini
From the kitchen of Antonio Petruzzi

SERVES 4

1 octopus (about 1¼ pounds/
    600 g)

For the pesto
7 ounces/200 g fagiolini
    (green beans)
¼ cup/60 ml extra-virgin
    olive oil
1 clove garlic, peeled
Salt and pepper
A small handful of
    fresh mint

4 medium-size waxy
    potatoes, peeled

Cook the octopus in a saucepan of boiling water for approximately 1½ hours.

Prepare the pesto by steaming the fagiolini beans for 5 to 8 minutes so they don't lose their color. Leave a handful of beans whole for serving, then take the rest and put them in a blender or food processor with the oil, garlic, salt and pepper to taste, and mint. Blend until the mixture is a coarse paste. Let stand until you are ready to assemble the dish.

In a saucepan of water, boil the potatoes for 15 to 20 minutes, leaving them al dente. Remove them from the water with a slotted spoon, let them cool, and then slice them into circles. Cut the tentacles from the octopus body and remove anything you find inside the body, including the plastic-like quill. Cut the head off the body and remove the bony beak if still attached. Cut the octopus body and the tentacles into pieces and season with salt and pepper to taste. Preheat the grill or griddle pan to hot and grill the octopus for a few minutes. Transfer to a plate and keep the octopus warm while you then cook the sliced potatoes. Add a glug of olive oil to the pan and quickly sear each side of the potatoes for a minute or two, until they are pale gold.

Place the potatoes on a plate, arrange the octopus on top, and use a spoon to pour the pesto over the top. Scatter the reserved fagiolini beans over the top.

Kebabs

MAKES 8 KEBABS

1 large zucchini, cut into
    rough chunks
1 block halloumi cheese, cut
    into chunks (or 9 ounces/
    250 g skinless, boneless
    chicken breast, cut into
    chunks)
1 large red onion, peeled
    and cut into chunks
9 ounces/250 g cherry
    tomatoes (or 1 red bell
    pepper, cut into chunks)

For the dressing
1 cup/250 g plain yogurt
¼ cup/25 g sliced almonds
1 clove garlic, peeled and
    coarsely chopped
A handful of fresh cilantro
A small handful of fresh
    mint
Juice of ½ lemon
1 tablespoon olive oil

If using wooden skewers, soak 8 skewers for 1 hour in cold water. Preheat the grill or broiler.

Assemble the vegetables and cheese on the skewers, alternating pieces of zucchini, halloumi, onion, and whole tomatoes. Leave the skewers to the side.

To make the dressing, put all the ingredients in a blender and blitz until smooth. You can pour this over the skewers before or after cooking them.

Put the skewers on the grill or under the broiler and cook for about 10 minutes, turning occasionally. *Pictured on page 206.*

Raw golden beets with cayenne and lime

Slice the beets as finely as possible into whisper-thin rounds. Assemble onto a really pretty plate. With dry fingers, sprinkle the cayenne pepper on top, then add a healthy squeeze of lime juice and, if you are so moved, a pinch of grated lime zest.

SERVES 2 OR 3

3 golden beets, washed and peeled

½ teaspoon cayenne pepper

1 lime, halved

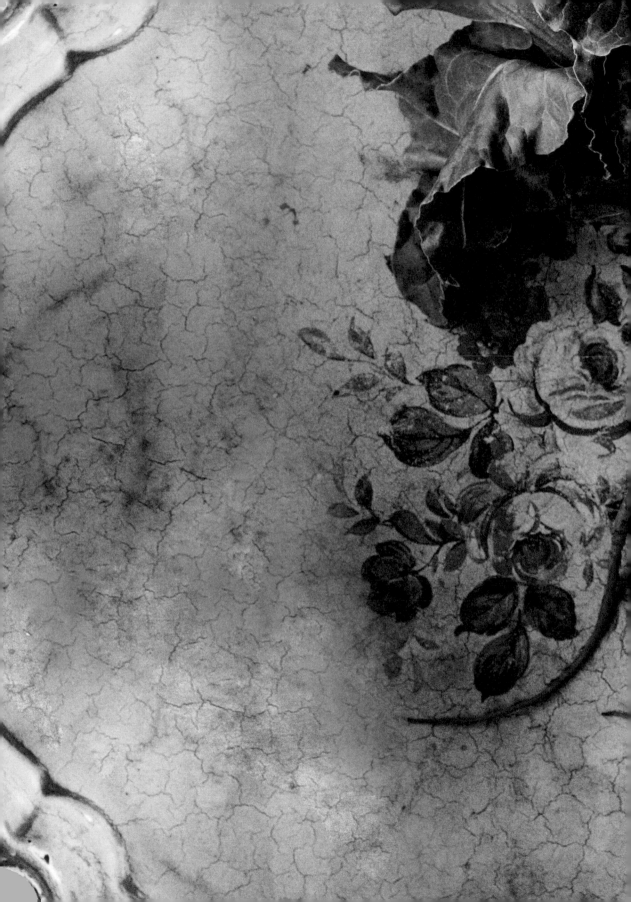

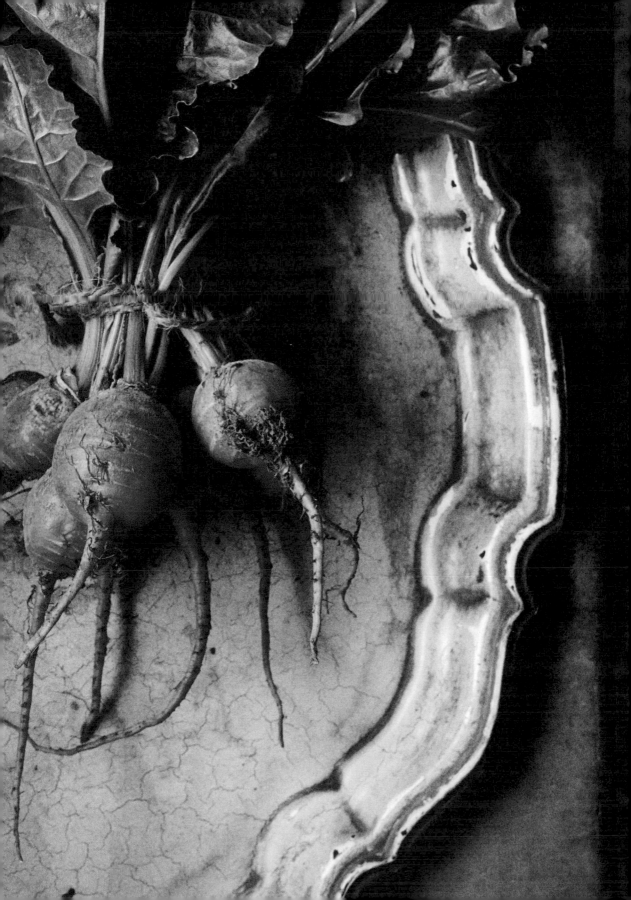

Summer
Suppers

Ricotta tarts with creamy pecorino sauce and shavings of black truffle

Tortino "soffiato" di ricotta con vellutata di pecorino e scaglie di tartufo nero

Another of Antonio Petruzzi's creations

Preheat the oven to 325°F/160°C. Grease 4 large or 6 small ramekins and set them aside.

To make the tarts, in a bowl, mix the ricotta with the egg whites, then add the Parmesan and a pinch of salt and pepper.

Pour the mixture into the prepared ramekins and bake for 20 minutes.

In the meantime, to make the sauce, heat the Pecorino and half-and-half in a glass bowl over a pan of simmering water, whisking well until the cheese is melted and the sauce is smooth. Add salt and pepper to taste.

Shave the truffle using a vegetable peeler.

Take the tarts out of the oven. You can serve the tarts in their ramekins, or you can refrigerate them for an hour or two, and, just before serving, gently run a palette knife around the edge while inverting them onto individual serving plates. Drench the tarts with the creamy sauce and decorate with as much black truffle as you like!

SERVES 4 TO 6

For the tarts
14 ounces/400 g sheep's
    milk ricotta cheese
4 egg whites
¾ cup/80 g grated
    Parmesan cheese
Salt and pepper
1 ounce/30 g black truffle

For the Pecorino sauce
1 cup/100 g grated aged
    Pecorino cheese
Generous ½ cup/150 ml
    half-and-half
Salt and pepper

Summer chicken stew

SERVES 4 TO 6

3 tablespoons olive oil
1 small chicken, chopped into pieces by your butcher
1 onion, peeled and finely chopped
2 cloves garlic, peeled and finely chopped
1 teaspoon ground turmeric
1 cup/250 ml white wine
1 cinnamon stick
1 bay leaf
Juice of 1 lemon
1 cup/250 ml chicken stock
1 can (14 ounces/400 g) chickpeas, drained and rinsed
¼ cup/25 g pitted black olives
Lemon wedges, for serving

A summery staple. Serve with rice or quinoa. It's much better the next day, as most soups and stews tend to be.

Heat 2 tablespoons of the olive oil in a large casserole over medium heat. Add the chicken pieces and brown, cooking for 10 to 15 minutes to brown evenly. Remove the chicken from the pot and keep to one side. Using the same pot, add the remaining oil and sweat the onion and garlic with the turmeric. After a few minutes, pour the wine over, add the cinnamon stick, bay leaf, and lemon juice, then add the chicken. Cook this for around 30 minutes, pouring in the stock little by little. Stir in the chickpeas and olives after 20 minutes and serve with lemon wedges.

Roasted tomato soup with basil oil

Roasting the tomatoes first gives an extraordinary creamy depth to this soup. Even without mascarpone, this soup is still gloriously decadent. This is also good cold, with a wallop of Greek yogurt or crème fraîche in place of the mascarpone and lots of black pepper.

Preheat the oven to 375°F/190°C. Place the tomatoes, onion, red bell pepper, and garlic in a roasting pan. Season with salt and pepper, splash with olive oil, and sprinkle over the sugar. Roast for around 45 minutes.

Take the pan out of the oven and allow to cool. Peel the onion and squeeze the garlic cloves from their skins. Place the onion, garlic, tomatoes, and bell pepper into a blender in batches, depending on the size of your blender, and purée until soft and velvety. When you have a soup, pour it into a large saucepan over low heat, add a spoonful of olive oil, and stir through the mascarpone. Heat for a minute or two.

Wash out the blender, place the basil and a tablespoon of olive oil in there, and blend on high. Put a swirl of this green mix through the soup just before serving.

SERVES 4

2¼ pounds/1 kg plum tomatoes, halved
1 large onion, quartered
1 large red bell pepper, seeded and quartered
4 cloves garlic
Salt and pepper
Olive oil
1 scant teaspoon dark brown sugar
1 tablespoon mascarpone cheese
A handful of fresh basil

Zucchini flower risotto

8 zucchini flowers with
   baby zucchini attached
2 tablespoons olive oil,
   plus extra for serving
1 clove garlic, peeled and
   finely chopped
1 small onion, peeled and
   finely chopped
2 cups/400 g arborio rice
6½ cups/1.5 liters hot
   chicken, beef, or
   vegetable stock
¼ cup/60 ml white wine
1 cup/100 g grated
   Parmesan cheese
Salt and pepper
A handful of chopped
   fresh basil

There is something hopelessly cheerful about zucchini flowers, and they are sweetly adaptable fellows, too. *Pictured on page 223*.

Detach the flowers from the zucchini, remove the stamens, and gently wipe the flowers clean. Slice the zucchini into thin rounds.

In a large risotto pan or a large heavy-bottomed pan, heat the olive oil over low heat, and sauté the garlic and onion until softened. Add the flowers and stir for a minute. Put in the rice and coat with the oil, stirring for a minute or so. Pour on a ladleful of stock and stir until it has been absorbed. Repeat this process for about 15 minutes, and then add the zucchini rounds and stir through. Add the white wine, stirring all the while. Cook for another 5 minutes and take off the heat, adding half of the Parmesan. Season and serve in low bowls with a drizzle of olive oil, the remaining grated Parmesan, and chopped basil.

Knife

○ FORK

+ peas.

Miso black colin

For the marinade
1 cup/150 g white
 miso paste
2 tablespoons sake
2 tablespoons mirin
1 tablespoon dark brown
 sugar
1 teaspoon tamari (wheat-
 free soy sauce)

4 pollack fillets (about
 7 ounces/200 g each)

Among many fish whose names are familiar to us, cod is being overfished and depleted. This is a fact and a cause for very real concern. There are many other fish similar in taste and texture to cod that are sustainable and which you can eat with a clear conscience (for a full list, check the Marine Stewardship Council website at www.msc.org). One of them is pollack. An English supermarket, obviously fearing that the public would be turned off by the name pollack—which seems to me to be a perfectly reasonable name—chose to rechristen the fish colin (the French name for hake). Yes. So here is a recipe for Miso Black Colin, and imagine the posh diners at Nobu ordering one of those please.

Put all of the marinade ingredients into a saucepan and heat over medium heat, stirring until all the sugar has melted. Bring to a boil, stir, and take off the heat. Leave to the side until totally cooled.

Wash and dry the fish. The next step is up to you, but I tend to put the marinade into a couple of resealable plastic bags, put two fish fillets in each, shake them up to make sure the fish is saturated with the miso, then leave in the fridge overnight. You can also just put the fillets in a shallow dish, pour the marinade on top and leave, covered, in the fridge for a few hours, but the overnight magic is worth it.

Preheat the broiler so that it's searing hot and put the fish on a broiler pan, pouring any excess marinade on the top. Broil for about 3 minutes on each side. Serve with some rice and a salad of cucumbers and shredded green onions.

HANGMAN'S SUPPERS

What do people choose to eat when their number is up? It's a subject I have always been fascinated by. Perhaps unsurprisingly, comfort food, for the most part. In parts of the United States where the death penalty is continued, correctional facility websites provide a macabre insight by listing the last-supper wishes of the condemned. These lists are testimony to childhoods bygone, straight out of a fifties sitcom: fried chicken, grilled cheese, brisket, hamburgers, spare ribs, onion rings, biscuits, mashed potatoes, pecan pie, cheesecake, malted milkshakes, and vanilla ice cream. Candies creep in too—Jolly Ranchers and chocolate bars abound. Though thoroughly limited by their circumstance and place of incarceration, the prisoners are given one last flight in culinary geography. The list dips from the Iowan corn-fed to Tex-Mex (refried beans and enchiladas, quesadillas and stuffed peppers) to the pungent memory of a mother's Caribbean pepperpot stew served with a side of ackee and saltfish.

Mercifully, an imagined last supper is a hell of a lot easier to get your head around. Chefs are always a good lot to plumb on the topic because they spend a great deal of time thinking about what they're going to eat next, or in this case, last. Once again, the food of childhood seems to win hands down, with Gordon Ramsay, April Bloomfield, and Heston Blumenthal all plumping for roast beef and potatoes; Nigella, a lemon roast chicken with creamed spinach, peas à la française, fennel salad, roast potatoes, chips *and* mashed potatoes (I love her); Jamie Oliver, spaghetti and, for pudding, a creamy rice one; and for Raymond Blanc, a shoulder of wild boar steeped in an herby red-wine jus à la maman. There was a lot of talk of cheese for dessert, too. Hugh Fearnley-Whittingstall is adamant his last supper is to be a breakfast, and it is splendidly specific. Scrambled eggs on Granary toast with bacon (fatty, nice and crisp, but not cremated, with the rind still on) and mushrooms fried in the bacon fat. All washed down with several strong cups of tea (milk and one sugar).

"I'd have to cook it myself," he says, "and make the tea, too. After that, I'd have a crisp, tart apple, ideally an Ashmead's Kernel."

I vacillate with mine. Sometimes it's achingly simple—a poached egg on toast with some pan-fried wild mushrooms on the side, mixed in perhaps with a little butter and some tarragon, garlic, and parsley; or a summer pea soup, with a swirl of mint and crème fraîche. Other times, it's the thing that would finish me off before anyone else could. A hearty French onion soup laden with Gruyère and bread, followed by a risotto perfumed with truffles, or a crispy skate wing with some potatoes dauphinoise. Dessert would have to be chocolate, the more molten the better— River Café's Chocolate Nemesis maybe, or a chocolate pot with some brandied cherries lurking in the bottom. At the moment though, written on a rainy day, I think it would be a mound of buttery mashed potatoes with some smoked haddock and a soft poached egg on top, covered in a creamy mustard sauce. But there's also kedgeree, or a thin-crust pizza, charred and sweet with a pool of mozzarella and some fiery chile oil, or a peanut butter–chocolate milkshake. You see the dilemma. Then I remember Le Café Anglais in Paddington, home to some of the finest food in England. The anchovy and Parmesan custard is the best comfort food, but with none of the stodgy predictability of comfort food. It is rich and grown-up, mysteriously puddingy. It is so good it makes me feel shy. Clever Rowley Leigh.

I think Dustin Hoffman came up with the best back-to-basics hangman's supper ever: mother's milk.

"Might as well go out as you came in," he mused, in gravel tones.

Rowley Leigh's Parmesan custard with anchovy toast and an herb salad (all mine)

Preheat the oven to 300°F/150°C. Lightly butter eight ⅓-cup/80-ml ramekins and put to the side.

To make the custards, mix the half-and-half, milk, and all but a tablespoon of the cheese in a bowl and warm gently over a pan of boiling water until the cheese has melted. Allow to cool completely before whisking in the egg yolks, a pinch of salt, finely ground white pepper, and a little cayenne. Divide the mixture among the prepared ramekins. Place the ramekins in a roasting pan or baking dish, pour in enough boiling water to come about halfway up the ramekins, and cover with buttered parchment paper. Bake for 15 minutes, or until the custards have just set.

To make the toasts, mash the anchovies and butter to a smooth paste and spread over four of the slices of bread (it's best if the bread is sliced very thinly). Cover with the remaining bread and toast in a sandwich press or panini machine.

To make the salad, coarsely chop the dill and mint and mix in a bowl with the arugula. Pour over the olive oil and lemon juice and toss with your fingers.

Sprinkle the remaining Parmesan over the warm custards and brown gently under a hot broiler. Cut the toasted anchovy sandwiches into little fingers and serve alongside the custards with the herb salad.

SERVES 4 (OR 8 AS A STARTER)

For the Parmesan custards
1¼ cups/300 ml half-and-half
1¼ cups/300 ml milk
1 cup/100 g finely grated Parmesan cheese
4 egg yolks
Salt and white pepper
Cayenne pepper

For the anchovy toasts
12 anchovy fillets
4 tablespoons/50 g unsalted butter
8 slices pain de campagne

For the herb salad
A handful of fresh dill
A handful of fresh mint
A handful of arugula
1 tablespoon olive oil
A squeeze of lemon juice

Fava bean risotto

SERVES 6

2 cups/300 g shelled fresh
    or frozen fava beans
1 tablespoon olive oil
2 tablespoons butter
1 small onion, peeled and
    finely chopped
1 clove garlic, peeled and
    finely chopped
2 cups/400 g Arborio rice
½ cup/125 ml white wine
5 cups/1.2 liters vegetable
    or chicken stock, hot
2 cups/100 g baby spinach
1 cup/100 g grated
    Pecorino cheese, plus
    extra for serving

There is something lovely and lulling about shelling fava beans at the kitchen table, stealing a few as you go. Another one of my favorite summer things is fava beans with sea salt, a hunk of Pecorino, and some chopped mint and olive oil. It is total perfection on its own. I guess this risotto is the graduation of that.

Bring a saucepan of salted water to a boil and cook the fava beans for 5 to 6 minutes. Drain and tip the beans into a bowl of cold water. Drain again, then pop each bean out of its skin and set aside.

In a risotto pan or heavy-bottomed saucepan, heat the olive oil and butter over lowish heat. Sweat the onion for a few minutes until translucent, then add the garlic, taking care it doesn't burn. Add the rice to the pan, giving it a good stir. Pour in the wine and cook until it's all been absorbed. Breathe.

Add the stock, ladle by ladle, stirring well between each addition and topping up only when the previous ladle has been absorbed. The trick to risotto is surrendering to the stirring, finding a calm in it. When the stock is used up, you're about there; it normally takes around 20 minutes. A few minutes before this point, stir in the fava beans, spinach, and Pecorino. Plate in low bowls, sprinkling with a bit more Pecorino.

Desserts

ROSES

I first went to India when I was twelve. We stayed in an ashram surrounded by mountains with pale pink stone floors and mango trees whose branches trailed the ground like old ladies' fingers. I loved everything about it. The dawn call to prayer, beating a solitary wail against the thick morning air; the sweet lassi that you had midmorning to keep you going, and at lunchtime; the trays piled high with rice, dal, and chapati. I loved the statues that peppered the landscape, all the gods from Hindu scriptures, among them cheeky Hanuman the monkey god and Ganesh the elephant with the little mouse who sat watchfully at his feet. My favorite was Lakshmi, the goddess of abundance, whose beauty and benevolence was protected from the elements by the stone shell in which she sat.

In the evening, we children were allowed to walk down the dirt road into the local village, where moon-eyed garlanded cows wandered in and out of people's yards and bats swooped so low that they could get caught in your hair if your hair was long enough. I wore mine up in a French plait because I had heard the shriek of the tall thirteen-year-old whose mother had spent hours armed with scissors and an iron will as she tried to release the clumsy bat from her daughter's thick nest of curls. The thought of those wings beating against my head made me shiver, and I stooped on these twilight walks, hair tight and unwelcoming.

The village had an unmistakable smell to it: bonfires, incense, raw gasoline, jasmine, dung, and rose water. It was heady and alien and crept around you like smoke. We passed the fishermen on the bridge and the dhobi washerman's shop, where, if you took your underclothes, they laughed at you, and we walked by the sadhu, who had rheumy eyes and stood ruler-straight, never seeming to move.

The sweet stall was run by a woman whose generous flesh fell over the folds of her tight orange sari, with a thick black coil of hair that any bat would be fool to invade. She smiled when she saw our greedy eyes and said, "Good evening, good evening."

"Good evening, Ma!" we chorused, grubby rupee notes unfurling from hot hands.

Her wares sat in paper cases stained with ghee. Carrot and pistachio halva and coconut *burfi*, and below, swimming in stainless steel bowls, were my very own downfall, the sloppy milk fed nursery desserts. The celestial *rasmalai* in a sweet wave of condensed milk— fat orange dumplings bobbing in a pure sugar syrup, *gulab jamun* to the uninitiated. The other marvel was a pale concoction seemingly dreamed up by the deities—vermicelli *kheer*, which sang of cardamom, rose water, and almonds.

A pudding that actually tasted of roses—what a thing!

It wasn't until years later when I was an adult with my own kitchen that I tried to mimic the rosy alchemy that I tasted in India. Rather than using rose water, I experimented with the real thing— some fat, blowsy, pink tea roses in the height of their bloom. Because English summers are often so horribly unpredictable, I suggest making the following and putting it in the freezer so that you have it at the ready for one of those of those rare halcyon Indian summer nights when the garden is ripe, voluptuous, and welcoming. And if you don't have a garden, you can simply conjure up some tea lights, throw open the windows, and put a thick picnic rug on the floor. To enhance the mood further, a soundtrack of bhangra or, for the more mellow, the sitar strains of Ravi Shankar.

Marbled rose petal ice cream

To make the rose petal jam, pour the sparkling rosé and sugar into a saucepan over low heat. Add the rose petals and keep stirring until the sugar has dissolved. Using a slotted spoon, remove three-quarters of the rose petals and set aside. Carry on reducing the sugar syrup over medium heat until thick and syrupy. Allow the jam to cool.

In a mixing bowl, whisk the sugar and egg yolks until pale in color, and keep to the side.

In a saucepan, heat the milk and cream until they reach boiling point. Remove from the stove. Whisking the whole time, temper the egg mixture and bring it up to the same temperature as the cream by adding the milk and cream mixture slowly. Add the reserved rose petals. Allow the custard to cool, and then remove the rose petals with a slotted spoon.

Pour the custard into your ice cream maker with half of the rose petal jam and churn as per the instructions. (If you do not have an ice cream maker, freeze the mixture in a plastic container for 2 hours. Remove from the freezer, transfer to a blender or food processor, and whiz for a minute or two. Pour back into the container. Freeze for another 2 hours.) Take the ice cream out of the machine or container and swirl the remaining rose petal jam roughly through the ice cream to make a marbled pink surface. Place in the freezer to set.

SERVES 4

For the rose petal jam
2 cups/500 ml sparkling rosé
¼ cup/40 g superfine sugar
¾ cup/20 g fragrant red or pink rose petals, washed

½ cup/125 g superfine sugar
8 egg yolks
2 cups/500 ml milk
2 cups/500 ml heavy cream

Chocolate meringue cookies

MAKES ABOUT 15 COOKIES

3 egg whites

A pinch of cream of tartar

½ cup/100 g superfine sugar

7 ounces/200 g dark chocolate, chopped

½ cup/60 g good-quality cocoa (natural or Dutch-processed), plus extra, to dust

I love chocolate meringue, hopefully with some sorbet, ice cream, or bashed-up raspberries and cream involved. These are glossy and easy and very good. *Pictured on page 239.*

Preheat the oven to its lowest setting. Line a baking sheet with parchment paper.

In a very clean bowl, whisk the egg whites until frothy, and then add the cream of tartar. Carry on whisking the whites until they are at the stiff-peak stage, and then, very slowly, add the sugar, a tablespoon at a time.

In a heatproof bowl over a saucepan of boiling water, melt the chocolate and sift the cocoa into the mix. Stir to combine. When the chocolate is smooth and glossy, slowly fold it into the glossy meringue.

Pipe or spoon the chocolate meringue onto the prepared baking sheet. Place in the oven for 45 to 55 minutes. When the meringues have cooled, dust with more cocoa.

Pineapple and mint granita

During my first trimester of pregnancy, I craved pineapple, particularly in this form. I dreamt of it, and carried whole pineapples up to bed with me, hacking into them in the night like some rotund jungle explorer. There is something about the sweet, refreshing coolness of pineapple mixed with the mint that banishes morning sickness, and for that I am thankful. *Pictured on page 243.*

SERVES 4 TO 6

2 pineapples, skin removed, fruit cut into chunks
2 sprigs fresh mint
Agave nectar or sugar, to sweeten (optional)

Place the pineapple chunks in the food processor and whiz until you have mostly juice. Strain the pineapple juice through a fine sieve. This makes around 2 cups/500 ml of juice. You can use store-bought pineapple juice if you like, but fresh pineapple is pretty spectacular.

In a heatproof bowl, pour a little boiling water over the mint sprigs. Remove the sprigs and run immediately under ice-cold water. Chop the mint finely and stir it into the strained pineapple juice. Taste and add agave or sugar if you think you should.

Freeze in a shallow metal container for around 2 hours. Check on it and use a fork to break up what should be shards of icy pineapple mixture. Once you've broken it up, refreeze again for a few hours.

Using a fork, scrape the granita into glasses and serve.

Poached winter fruits with crème anglaise

This works as a lighter dessert after a hearty meal, but you could just as well serve it alongside a Christmassy breakfast. And you can totally play around with the fruit you use. *Pictured on page 247.*

Poach the fruits in a large saucepan with enough water to just cover the fruit (a scant cup). Start with the quince, poaching for around 8 minutes over medium heat, and then add the pears and apples and cook for another 5 minutes. Finally, add the figs and plums and poach for 5 minutes more.

In a separate saucepan, mix the wine, sugar, cinnamon, bay leaf, cloves, star anise, and orange slices and bring to a boil. Simmer for 10 to 15 minutes. When both the poached fruit and the wine syrup have cooled, pour the syrup over the fruit and leave covered overnight in the refrigerator.

Make the crème anglaise shortly before serving. In a saucepan, bring the milk and vanilla bean and seeds to a boil, take off the heat, and allow to infuse for about 10 minutes. In a heatproof bowl, whisk together the egg yolks and the sugar, and place the bowl over a saucepan of boiling water. Whisk briskly. Gradually strain the vanilla milk in to the yolk mixture and continue to stir as the custard thickens. Take off the heat and serve over your fruit. Serve this in one big beautiful glass bowl—it's good either cold or warm.

SERVES 4

For the poached fruit
1 quince, peeled, cored, and quartered
2 pears, peeled, cored, and quartered
2 apples, peeled, cored, and quartered
2 figs, quartered
2 plums, pitted and quartered
2 cups/500 ml fruity red wine
½ cup/100 g superfine sugar
1 cinnamon stick
1 bay leaf
A few cloves
1 star anise
A few orange slices

For the crème anglaise
A generous ½ cup/150 ml full-fat milk
1 vanilla bean, slit in half and seeds scraped
4 egg yolks
¼ cup/50 g superfine sugar

Uncle's chocolate soufflés with brandied cherries

Ned, who is seventeen, is my littlest brother. He is divine. At six foot three and still growing, he is not little; he is like a long bean. For some meandering reason, my other brother and sister and I call him "Uncle." Whenever we see him, we sing a very annoying Uncle theme song to him to the tune of "Let's Get Ready to Rumble" and, understandably, it drives him a little insane. I think he may end up a politician. He has always been quite particular when it comes to food. Onions are banished, as is garlic, and mushrooms don't get a look in. He does, however, like chocolate. This chocolate soufflé, then, is for him, but perhaps without the brandied cherries (which I'm imagining he might be appalled by). His version would probably have ice cream.

Preheat the oven to 300°F/150°C. Using a knob of butter, grease the inside of four small ramekins.

Place your chocolate in a heatproof bowl over a saucepan of boiling water. Stir the chocolate so it melts evenly. Keep over low heat. In a very clean dry bowl, whip the egg whites. I do this in my electric mixer as it makes life very easy. When the egg whites are glossy and stiffening, start adding the sugar, bit by bit.

Take your chocolate off the heat and whisk the egg yolks into it. Very gently, add the chocolate to the egg whites. The key is to fold rather than mix or whisk because you want the whites to stay as light as a feather. *Gently* divide among the ramekins, smoothing the edges with your thumb, which will help them rise. Place the ramekins on a baking sheet, place in the oven, and don't you open that door for 20 minutes! Serve immediately.

To distract from soufflé anxiety, make the cherries while the soufflés bake. In a small saucepan, combine the cherries with the brandy, sugar, and water. Cook over low to medium heat for about 10 minutes, or until the cherries are soft and sloppy, but still holding their basic shape. Serve alongside your beauteous soufflés.

SERVES 4

3½ ounces/100 g really
   good-quality dark
   chocolate, chopped
4 egg whites
¼ cup/50 g superfine sugar
2 egg yolks

For the brandied cherries
A handful of pitted
   cherries
1 tablespoon brandy
1 tablespoon sugar
⅓ cup/80 ml water

Earl Grey and lavender ice cream

SERVES 4

1 tablespoon chopped fresh lavender leaves

4 tablespoons Earl Grey tea leaves

8 egg yolks

½ cup/125 g superfine sugar

2 cups/500 ml heavy cream

2 cups/500 ml milk

Dried lavender flowers, to garnish

Earl Grey works beautifully with lavender. You can also make a wonderful iced tea using Earl Grey, lavender, and simple syrup, steeping and leaving in the fridge to cool. *Pictured on page 250.*

First, enclose the lavender and Earl Grey tea leaves in a piece of cheesecloth and secure with kitchen string. Make sure the string is tightly knotted. Put to one side.

In a mixing bowl, whisk the egg yolks and sugar until pale and creamy and keep to one side.

In a heavy-bottomed saucepan, heat the cream, milk, and the bouquet of lavender and tea leaves up until boiling point, and then remove from the heat.

Temper the egg and sugar mixture by slowly adding the infused cream to bring the egg up to the same temperature, whisking all the time. Strain the mixture and then allow it to cool.

Churn in your ice cream maker as per the instructions. (If you do not have an ice cream maker, freeze the mixture in a plastic container for 2 hours. Remove from the freezer, transfer to a blender or food processor and whiz for a minute or two. Pour back into the container.) Freeze for another 2 hours, then serve, sprinkled with lavender flowers.

Rice pudding cake

This is a risotto cake of sorts. It was made for me by an Italian mama in Sorrento, and the recipe was mimed in a clamoring kitchen. I think that it has worked regardless!

Preheat the oven to 325°F/160°C

Into a large saucepan on the stovetop, pour the milk and then add the rice. Add to this the orange zest and cook over low heat, stirring frequently, until the rice has absorbed all the milk. This should take around 15 minutes. Take the pan off the heat and let cool.

When the milky rice has cooled, mix in the sugar, eggs, butter, raisins, and almonds. Grease a 9-inch springform pan and sprinkle with half of the crushed amaretti biscuits.

Pour the rice mixture into the pan and bake for around 45 minutes. When the cake is golden on top, remove from the oven and let cool for at least an hour. Gently slide the cake from the springform pan onto a serving plate. To serve, dust with the remaining crushed amaretti biscuits and orange zest. This is also heaven if it's been in the fridge for a few hours.

SERVES 4

4 cups/1 liter milk
¾ cup/160 g Arborio rice
Grated zest of 1 orange, plus extra to decorate
½ cup/150 g superfine sugar
3 eggs
2 tablespoons butter
¼ cup/50 g raisins
½ cup/50 g sliced almonds
4 tablespoons crushed amaretti biscuits

Almost mother-in-law cake

SERVES 4 TO 6

1½ cups/300 g butter, very soft

2 cups/500 g superfine sugar

4 eggs

3 cups/350 g all-purpose flour, sifted

Generous ½ cup/75 g natural cocoa, sifted

2 teaspoons baking powder

2 teaspoons vanilla extract

½ cup/125 ml milk, at room temperature

½ cup/125 ml boiling water

Juice and finely grated zest of 1 orange

1 cup/120 g chopped walnuts, plus extra to decorate

Shredded candied orange zest, to decorate

For the chocolate icing

9 ounces/250 g good-quality dark chocolate, chopped

1 cup/250 ml heavy cream

This recipe was sent to me by a reader named Sabine. It was passed on to her by her "almost mother-in-law," to whom we are spectacularly grateful. "Almost weddings" can wax and wane, but chocolate cake is here to stay, and this one, like Sabine, is lovely, the orange and walnuts happy bedfellows. *Pictured on page 255.*

Preheat the oven to 350°F/180°C. Line a 10-inch/25-cm cake pan with parchment paper.

In a large bowl, mix together everything (except the extra walnuts and candied orange zest), one after another, in the order they are listed. Beat until smooth and pour into the prepared cake pan. Bake for about 1 hour. Remove the cake from the oven, and let cool for at least an hour. Turn out the cake onto a serving plate (use a palette knife if you need help, but the parchment paper should make this easy).

To make the icing, place the chocolate in a heatproof bowl over a saucepan of boiling water. Stir the chocolate so it melts evenly. Bring the cream to a boil in a small saucepan, then pour over the chocolate. Stir occasionally until smooth and glossy.

Thickly spread/swirl the icing over the top and sides of the cake with an icing spatula and top with the extra walnuts and candied orange zest.

Panettone bread-and-butter pudding

Bread-and-butter pudding is an English staple, proper nursery food. This is a good one for Christmastime when you want a hearty, warming pudding—panettone makes it a bit more interesting and festive. *Pictured on pages 258–259.*

Preheat the oven to 375°F/190°C.

Whisk together the half-and-half, milk, and eggs. Slice the vanilla bean in half and scrape the seeds into the egg and cream mixture. Add the superfine sugar and whisk some more.

Slice the panettone into thick slices and butter each slice. Arrange the buttered panettone slices in an ovenproof dish. Scatter with the apple and sprinkle with the nutmeg. Pour over the half-and-half mixture and make sure the panettone is evenly soaked. Sprinkle the top with the brown sugar.

Bake for 20 to 30 minutes or until golden and crispy. Serve hot.

SERVES 10

2½ cups/600 ml half-and-half
1¾ cups/450 ml milk
3 eggs
1 vanilla bean
½ cup/150 g superfine sugar
1 medium-sized panettone
Butter, for spreading
1 apple, peeled, cored, and finely diced
A pinch of freshly grated nutmeg
¼ cup/50 g brown sugar

Coconut sorbet

SERVES 2 TO 4

Generous ½ cup/150 g
    superfine sugar
¾ to 1 cup/185 to 250 ml
    water
½ cup/125 ml coconut milk
 Juice of ½ lime
½ cup/40 g shredded
    dried coconut

For me, this is up there with Pineapple and Mint Granita (page 241). You can skip the lime if you are not a fan, but it gives this sorbet a lovely sharp edge.

Place the sugar in a heavy-bottomed saucepan. Add the water and simmer for 5 minutes, making a syrup. Stir in the coconut milk and lime juice. Add the shredded coconut and allow the mixture to cool.

Churn in your ice cream maker as per the instructions. (If you do not have an ice cream maker, freeze the mixture in a plastic container for 2 hours. Remove from the freezer, transfer to a blender, and whiz for a minute or two. Pour back into the container.) Freeze for another 2 hours, then serve.

Ruby Frais strawberry semifreddo

This recipe is so titled for a young girl named for a future of all things sweet, a Miss Ruby Frais. Her dad calls her "Pudding" and she, like me, is partial to berries and vanilla ice cream. This then, quite literally, has her name all over it. *Pictured on page 262.*

Put the strawberries in a bowl. Tip the sugar on top and leave to macerate for 1 hour. When they're a lovely, sticky mess, pour into a blender or food processor with the lemon juice and purée.

In a large bowl, whip the cream until thick but soft enough to fall from the spoon. Pour the fruit into the cream and fold through thoroughly.

Put into a 9- by 5-inch/23- by 13-cm loaf pan. Freeze for about 1 hour until crystals form around the edges, then transfer the mixture to the blender or food processor and whiz for a minute or two. Return the mixture to the loaf pan and freeze for 2 hours, blend again, then freeze for around 4 hours.

Take out 20 minutes before serving. You can slice it directly in the loaf pan or turn out the semifreddo and slice it on a plate. Scatter meringues and extra strawberries over each serving.

SERVES 4

1 pound/450 g strawberries, hulled and halved, plus extra for serving

¾ cup/100 g confectioners' sugar

Juice of ½ small lemon

1¼ cups/300 ml heavy cream

10 ounces/30 g meringue cookies, bashed up

THE NUTCRACKER

I wrote this story for Waitrose Food Illustrated *magazine to go with a Christmas Syllabub recipe that I created for a December issue. They asked me to write a modern take on* The Nutcracker *and gave me quite a small word count in which to do it.*

Here it is. I hope you like it.

It was Christmas Eve. In a spindly house perched in a row of other spindly houses, a girl with moist sugar plum eyes sat in a soft green chair. Her legs were thrown over the side, her shoes were scarlet ending in a rapier heel, and much to her mother's despair, if you squinted, you could see her knickers.

"Oh Maude," the mother said. "When will you sit like a lady?"

"My heart is broken," Maude said. "I will be ladylike when, and IF, I meet a MAN."

"Is this about that boy?" Maude's father groaned.

"The King Rat?" her little brother, Frederick, asked. "The one who snogged your friend Maxine at the dance?"

"Would you like to put the fairy on the top of the tree?" her mother said.

"Don't bother me with your pagan trifles. My heart is broken."

"Maude darling, do try and pull yourself together, your godfather will be here any minute. It's Christmas Eve. There will be many other boys. Could you try and summon a smile?"

Maude grimaced. The doorbell rang.

"Merry Christmas one and all!" Her godfather, M. Sousedalot, spun into the room on a sharp whisky breeze, his sandpaper voice grating the edges of Maude's misery.

"Frederick, for you dear, fat boy, a chocolate orange. And ah, Miss Heartbreak, for you, this—symbolic under the circumstances . . ."

It was a nutcracker.

"Uh, yeah, thanks?" Maude looked at her mother in appeal.

Fat Frederick (who wasn't normally allowed E numbers) ate his entire chocolate orange and got hyperactive.

"I want that nut man!" he said. "Mum, my present's gone and Maude still has hers."

He tried to snatch the nutcracker from Maude and, in the tussle, it slipped from his hot buttery hand. There was a crack as the nutcracker hit the floor. Half of his leg lay splintered beside him.

"Wow, Frederick. Has mum ever told you you're adopted?" Maude said.

After everyone had gone to bed, Maude lay under the Christmas tree listening to Wham's greatest hits, with the nutcracker in her hand. The King Rat had told her she was post-modern after he kissed her at the Fleet Foxes gig. What use post-modernism when she was alone under the mistletoe? She wondered. She shut her eyes. The clock chimed.

Shadows danced in her eyelids. Stealthy shadows wearing bosomy dresses and whispering, "Look at Maude! She's so innocent and dull! Pick me, pick me."

Maude opened her eyes and was greeted by an army of dancing rats in skinny jeans. Their horrible two-step was led by the King Rat himself, leering at her over Maxine's fake tanned shoulder. Dry ice swirled around them.

"Alright Maude," he said.

"Go away!" Maude cried.

Closer and closer they came, until she could smell Maxine's cheap perfume and see the angry cluster of spots beading the King Rat's whiskers.

"I never really liked you," Maxine said.

"Please leave me alone," Maude begged.

She heard the sound of creaking wooden joints. Through the dry ice she saw a red uniform, a beard, a tall black hat.

"Allow me," the Nutcracker said.

He marched through the dry ice, sending the rats scuttling in his wake. He felled the King Rat with one wooden blow. He hadn't bargained for Maxine though. She pulled out a bottle of hairspray from her bag and sprayed him squarely in the eyes. The Nutcracker stumbled drunkenly. Maude ran to him. As Maxine advanced, Maude took off her shoe and threw it at Maxine's beehive. It sliced through the middle like an arrow.

"My hair! You've ruined my hair," Maxine shrieked and fainted clean away.

Maude led the Nutcracker through the fog, holding his hand as the darkness enveloped them. Until . . .

There was snow; everywhere there was snow and light. Maude turned to the Nutcracker, whose flesh-and-blood hand she realized she was holding. The beard and vice-tight jaw had melted somehow, revealing laughing eyes and a clean (and distinctly rugged) jaw.

"Wow," Maude said, for the second time that night.

"Long story, involving a curse," the Nutcracker said. "Anyway, you've broken it, you goddess."

They had arrived at a shimmering sea, on which a boat bobbed towards them. The Nutcracker picked Maude up and flung her in. She braced herself, but landed on a nest of rose-scented, belly-rounded softness.

"But it's Turkish Delight!" Maude's eyes were round.

The icebergs they wove between were meringues; glossy and soft peaked. Dark chocolate seals slipped beneath the boat and chased each other. They sailed forth through geysers of thick, sweet cream and rock pools of salted caramel. Their compass was a sugar plum mermaid, her tail a beacon, leading them home . . .

"Maude, when I said you'd meet other boys, I didn't mean now this instant, under the Christmas tree!" It was morning. Maude's mother stood above her, looking dangerous.

"What?!" Maude woke in the drowsy embrace of a man in red uniform.

"Madam, I can explain everything," the Nutcracker said. "In the meantime—Turkish Delight?"

Christmas sugar plum syllabubby mess

SERVES 8

For the meringues
6 egg whites
1⅓ cups/340 g superfine
    sugar
A pinch of salt

For the rest
4 plums (about 9 ounces/
    250 g), pitted and
    coarsely chopped
4 pears, peeled, cored, and
    coarsely chopped
¼ cup/60 ml water
4 tablespoons runny
    honey or agave nectar
3 tablespoons superfine
    sugar
¾ cup/185 ml heavy cream
¾ cup/185 ml Greek yogurt
½ cup/50 g toasted sliced
    almonds

For charming men in uniform.
Or, for charming men, in uniform.

Start with the meringues. Preheat the oven to its lowest setting and line a baking sheet with parchment paper. In a very clean, dry bowl, whip the egg whites until they reach firm peaks. Gradually whisk in the sugar and salt until the mixture is a thick cloud of white. This should take somewhere around 8 minutes, and an electric mixer is a blessing unless you are very staunch.

Spoon the mixture into eight rounds, about a heaping tablespoon each, on the parchment paper and bake for 1 hour 15 minutes or so, until firm but not highly colored. Leave the meringues on a wire rack to cool.

To make the compote and syllabub, put the fruit in a small saucepan with the water and honey or agave over low heat. Cook the fruit for around 8 minutes or until it has softened. Pour the mixture through a sieve. Reserve the liquid and set the fruit aside.

Put the liquid back in the pan with the sugar and cook over low heat to make a syrup. This will take about 10 minutes. Reserve and cool. Chill the fruit for at least 1 hour.

In a bowl, whisk together the cream with a few tablespoons of the reserved fruit syrup. When the mixture begins to thicken, add the Greek yogurt and whisk some more. Now for the imaginative bit. Do you want individual servings or one big platter of meringues, with the fruit compote spooned on top and the cream and syrup spooned on top after that? Or, do you want to serve it in layers in individual colored glasses, with some toasted almonds on top? Picture the land of sweets, and go for it.

Armagnac apricot panna cotta

Panna cotta is basically baked cream. No one said it was good for you, but God, it's good. These are not baked, so are therefore bastardized panna cotta, but therein lies their ease and joy. I am a huge Armagnac fan. It works wonderfully for tarting up dried fruit—apricots, prunes, and plums—and it tastes very grown-up

First, soak the gelatin sheets in cold water to cover. They should be soft after about 10 minutes.

In a saucepan, mix together the cream, sugar, and vanilla bean and seeds and bring to a simmer, but not a boil. Remove from the heat. Lift the gelatin sheets out of the water, add them to the pan, and mix until they dissolve. Add the Armagnac, mix, and divide the mixture among four ramekins. Refrigerate for at least 4 hours.

While the panna cottas are setting, make the apricot compote. Place the apricots in a saucepan with the orange juice, Armagnac, and sugar. Stir and cook over low heat for 5 to 8 minutes. Keep to one side.

When you are about serve, take the panna cottas out of the fridge. Place the ramekins in a shallow basin filled with enough warm water to come halfway up the sides. Turn out each panna cotta onto a serving dish and serve surrounded with apricot compote.

SERVES 4

2 sheets gelatin
2 cups/500 ml heavy
  cream
½ cup/100 g superfine
  sugar
1 vanilla bean, slit in half
  and seeds scraped
1 tablespoon Armagnac

For the apricot compote
A small handful of dried
  apricots
½ cup/125 ml orange juice
1 tablespoon Armagnac
1 tablespoon superfine
  sugar

Acknowledgments and resounding thanks

My darling husband Jamie, you are everything that is good and right in the world. One day I will make poached eggs as beautifully as you do. Probably not though and breakfast wouldn't be half as fun.

My gorgeous family, pre-existing and the in-laws. Thank you for your recipes, stories, and sweetness, and for your abiding love. Clover and Luke, thank you for all the many fantasy food games through the years and thank you for the daily debriefs. Ned, thank you for being such a demon onion chopper. Benji, thank you for chickens cottaging, pregnant caretaking, chauffeuring, and happily sharing chocolate with me on the sofa while your brother is away. You rock.

A massive thank you to the food goddesses that continue to inspire and awe, sharing techniques, recipes and wisdom—Tiffany Crouch, Ginny Rolfe, and Alice Hart, you are all brilliant and I thank each one of you.

To the entire team at HarperCollins who make my life lovely and continue to make it all a pleasure. A huge thank you and big fat kiss to my wonderful editor Carole Tonkinson, Belinda Budge, Helen Hawksfield, Lee Motley, and Anna Gibson for your enduring kindness, humor, and attention to detail.

Thank you as ever to the creative team—to Jan Baldwin for your incredible photographs, skill, and fun; Patrick Budge for your seamless design and dead lions in the garden; Alice Hart for beauteous food, chatting, and morning sickness skills; Emma Thomas for your splendid props and eye; and Peter Dixon for being an all-round gent.

Thank you dear Grainne Fox for your unerring support, sagacity, and ability to sort things out, and a big hug and thank you to Mink Choi.

Thank you Angela Becker for getting it from the beginning and having unbelievable patience and resolve. Thank you *and* a squeeze to Catrina Naylor, fellow tour widow and logistics whiz.

My girlfriends—as always—thank you and much, much love.

SD

index

Suppliers

Porcelain tableware: Billy Lloyd, www.billyllloyd.co.uk
Ceramic tableware: Toast, www.toast.co.uk
Vintage napkins: The Cloth Shop, www.theclothshop.net
Garden table: Petersham Nurseries, www.petershamnurseries.com
Cressida Bell woodland fabric: Borderline, www.borderlinefabrics.com
Floral rococo fabric: Mulberry Home, www.mulberryhome.com
Flowers: Scarlet and Violet, www.scarletandviolet.co.uk

The author and publisher would like to thank Rowley Leigh and Le Café Anglais for permission to include their recipe for Parmesan Custard with Anchovy Toast and also Trina Hahnemann for the recipe Rye Cracker Breads with Horseradish and Smoked Trout Pâté.

SOPHIE DAHL began her career as a model, but writing was always her first love. In 2003 she wrote an illustrated novella called *The Man with the Dancing Eyes*, which was a *Times* bestselling book. This was followed by a novel, *Playing with the Grown-Ups*, published to widespread praise by Bloomsbury in 2007. Dahl is a contributing editor at British *Vogue*. She has also written for US *Vogue*, *Waitrose Food Illustrated* magazine, the *Observer*, the *Guardian*, and the *Saturday Times Magazine*, among others.

A devoted eater and cook, she wrote a book chronicling her misadventures with food, *Miss Dahl's Voluptuous Delights*, published by HarperCollins in 2009, which was her second *Times* bestseller. Following on the success of *Voluptuous Delights*, Dahl wrote and presented a popular BBC2 six-part cooking series, *The Delicious Miss Dahl*, which aired in numerous countries all over the world.

Dahl lives in England, where she continues to work on her journalism, fiction, and baking. Visit www.sophiedahl.com.